Martin Gostelow

JPMGUIDES

Contents

This Way China 3

Flashback 7

On the Scene 17

Beijing and the North 17

Xi'an and
the Silk Road 36

Nanjing and
the Yangtze 47

Kunming 62

Shanghai and
the Grand Canal 65

Guangzhou and
the South 77

Hong Kong 89

Macau 99

Cultural Notes 102

Shopping 106

Dining Out 109

The Hard Facts 114

Index 127

Maps

Yangtze 50–51, Li River 84,
Hong Kong Central District 90–91,
Guangzhou 122, Nanjing 123,
Shanghai 124, Xi'an 125, Macao 126

Fold-out map

China
Beijing, Hong Kong

This Way China

With its vast area and 1.3 billion people, the People's Republic of China is a land of infinite variety and wild contradictions. A score of modern cities compete to emulate Hong Kong's glittering skyline and economic dynamism, but farming methods have hardly changed for 2000 years; strawhatted peasants till the soil by hand or guide the plough behind a pair of lumbering water buffalo. When you fly over China, pick a window seat to see the passing panorama of intensively cultivated plains, rice-growing wetlands, rugged mountains and empty deserts. The scenic beauty of the great river valleys and dramatic gorges inspired a tradition of painting that you might think exaggerated, until you board a boat and see the reality.

The legendary sights you have come to see are truly unforgettable: the awe-inspiring Great Wall, the gorgeous palaces of Beijing's Forbidden City, the unique Terracotta Army of Xi'an. With pride in the past restored, archaeologists are uncovering new wonders all the time. Today's China is just as compulsive: the street scene and teeming throngs, the sounds and smells, people doing their morning *tai chi* exercises, playing dominoes, having a haircut. Markets and stores offer an endless range of arts and crafts at enticing prices, and the varied restaurants and food stalls make eating out an adventure.

Embracing Change

For most of its 4,000 years of recorded history, China was cut off from the rest of the world by mountains and deserts, or dangerous seas. The rulers of the Middle Kingdom, as they called it, were convinced that it was heaven's most favoured nation. Change was fiercely resisted until forced on them by the foreigners that they had despised as backward barbarians. The century from the Opium Wars to the foundation of the People's Republic in 1949 was a long nightmare of invasions, humiliations and civil war. Not surprisingly, the new regime viewed the rest of the world with suspicion verging on paranoia.

China is undergoing transformations that would have seemed unimaginable only a quarter of a century ago. The consumer boom that begain in the 1980s has put TV sets into over 90 per cent of homes. In the cities, the latest fashions have replaced drab uniform clothing, and the trendy young go clubbing. Chairman Mao must be spinning in his tomb. Very high taxes on cars, and low fares on public transport, are intended to discourage car ownership, but production is still mounting year by year. Rush hour jams these days are made up of more than buses and bicycles.

The most explosive growth has been in the special economic zones like Shenzhen near Hong Kong, packed with new factories producing for export. Here young people from poor rural areas crowd in to earn wages that may be minimal by world standards, but are more than they can hope for back in their home villages.

The young and well-educated have embraced the market economy with enthusiasm. The best and the brightest continue their studies in the West, and return with advanced degrees. A talent for business has always been part of the national character. Denied legal forms of expression for the first 40 years of communism, it has now been set free. The government implicitly offers a trade-off: increasing prosperity but severe restrictions on political activity. Village councils are the only representative bodies so far chosen by popular vote. Religious freedom, on the other hand, has been restored. Now that the Cultural Revolution is a distant, evil memory, people are no longer frightened of going to Buddhist or Taoist temples, or to the churches that have re-opened in the big cities. In fact, because so many places of worship were destroyed in that era, those that survived are usually packed, and the state seems unconcerned. Confucianism, not strictly a religion but an ethical code, was a special target of the Red Guards, but it's now positively favoured as the authorities worry about growing levels of corruption and bad behaviour.

The Great Divide

The gulf between the haves and the have-nots is enormous, and still growing as a result of the get-rich-quick era unleashed by Deng Xiaoping. At the top are the party bosses and a small elite of the well-connected; then the educated younger generation in the big cities who have tapped in to the new opportunities. Farmers with their own slice of good land are also doing well. Then comes the vast rural majority, 70 per cent of the population. For most, their life is still one of unremitting toil; those on the poorest land are barely able to scratch a living, even in a good year. At the bottom of the heap are the 100 million or so of the minorities—Tibetans, Uzbeks, Li, Mongolians and 50 other groups—many of them liv-

At Suzhou, as all over China, people get up at dawn to do their tai chi exercises.

ing in harsh climates on the periphery of China. Their average income per head is estimated at 20 US dollars a year. About 90 million are illiterate, mostly in the remoter areas where schools are poor. The education system is still suffering from the loss of morale following the persecution of teachers during the Cultural Revolution, and the greater attractions of a business career.

The Open Door

It has never been simpler to visit China. The authorities want to encourage tourism and there are few restrictions and few forbidden areas. You can get around with ease and speed; in the best hotels in the big cities, standards of service are as good as you will find anywhere in the world, and in smaller places you can still expect to find somewhere clean and pleasant to stay. Comfortable trains run on time between all the important cities. The latest airliners flying from brand-new airports connect the major centres, and regular services to far-flung provinces make it feasible to see widely scattered highlights, even in a short trip. In the remoter rural areas you'll still be the object of curiosity, but foreigners are becoming a familiar sight and they are sure of a friendly welcome.   5

STOP AT ONE

The baby boom of the 1950s and 60s, encouraged by Mao Zedong, took China's population past the 1,000 million mark. How were all those people to be fed, housed, employed? In 1980, the one-child policy was launched, enforced through loss of social benefits, maybe even of jobs, if parents have more. Some results are already clear. The average age rose from 28 to 33 in less than a decade. People are marrying later: 26 for men, 23 for women in urban areas. Doting parents turn their one and only into a "little emperor" (or empress); not only sociologists wonder what the long-term effects will be. The male:female ratio of births is 120:100, prompting the authorities to restrict sex identification in the womb. There will be more and more ageing dependants for each person at work, and China has no state pension. And the population is still rising, mainly due to greater life expectancy, but also because the policy doesn't apply to the minority ethnic groups, such as the Mongolians in the north, the Uighurs in the west and the Miao in the south.

Flashback

Beginnings

The longest surviving civilization in the world emerged in China more than 5,000 years ago. It already had a written language, based on pictograms, the forerunner of today's Chinese characters. The secret of weaving silk fabric from the thread produced by silk worms was probably discovered around 2000 BC, the time of the semi-mythical Xia dynasty. There's no such doubt about the Shang, who ruled the north China plain around the Yellow River from the 16th to the 11th centuries BC. Excavations have revealed their skill at bronze-casting and shown that jade was prized, as it still is today.

The Zhou state, which grew up near today's city of Xi'an, succeeded the Shang in about 1050 BC and established a feudal system to control extensive territories through the ruler's relations and vassals. Towards the end of the Zhou era, two of China's foremost thinkers, Confucius (Kong Fuzi) and Laozi (Lao Tse), proposed codes of conduct and belief that had far-reaching influence. The legendary Laozi (the name means Old Master) inspired the creed that came to be called Taoism. With its emphasis on spirit worship and fatalism in the face of cosmic forces, it became the dominant Chinese religion. Confucius, by contrast, did not concern himself with the supernatural but explored the realm of social interaction, propounding the virtues of honesty, benevolence, truth and brotherly respect. He would not have wished his teachings to be thought of as a religion, although some of his later followers treated them as such. His tomb, near his birthplace at Qufu in Shandong, became a place of pilgrimage, visited by many emperors over the centuries. During Mao Zedong's Cultural Revolution, Confucius was regarded as a "bourgeois" figure of hatred, and many Confucian temples were destroyed, but today he is widely revered.

While intellectual life was flourishing, politically the Zhou state was in decay. Its collapse around 475 BC ushered in the period of the Warring States, who divided and fought over the territory on and off for the next 250 years.

The Mighty Qin

Qin Shihuang took control of the Qin state in central China in 237 BC when he was 22, with a mission to conquer. By 221 he had created the first unified Chinese empire. Ruthless and efficient, he imposed a common written language, currency and laws. A highway system was built, and construction of the Great Wall began, paid for by extortionate taxation and using huge numbers of conscripted labourers. Ancient culture was suppressed; the only books that were permitted were favourable commentaries on the Qin regime and practical manuals. The rest were burned, and many scholars were killed.

The emperor spent much of his life travelling, first subduing and then defending his vast territories. He died on the road, in 210 BC, on his way to search for a mythical island where the inhabitants knew the secret of eternal life. His body was buried in the huge tomb near Xi'an which had been under construction since he came to the throne as a child; the celebrated terracotta warriors were his symbolic bodyguard. His successor failed to get a grip on the levers of power; within four years the empire had collapsed into civil war.

CHINESE CHRONOLOGY

Xia Dynasty	21st–16th centuries BC
Shang Dynasty	16th–11th centuries BC
Zhou Dynasty	11th–3rd centuries BC
Qin Dynasty	221–206 BC
Han Dynasty	206 BC–220 AD
Time of disunity	220–581
Sui Dynasty	581–618
Tang Dynasty	618–907
Song Dynasty	960–1279
Yuan (Mongolian) Dynasty	1279–1368
Ming Dynasty	1368–1644
Qing (Manchu) Dynasty	1644–1911
Republic of China	1912–1949
People's Republic	1949–

Han Era

The Han dynasty, which lasted from 206 BC to AD 220, was founded by a rebel Qin general, Liu Bang, with its capital at Chang'an (now Xi'an). The Han rulers continued the centralization of the state, but with less of the iron fist. They started nationwide examinations to fill positions in the civil service, introduced a single currency and standard coins, and encouraged scholarship and the arts. Hostile nomads to the north were kept at bay by punitive expeditions or payment in gold, and the national territory was enlarged to roughly the extent of China today. Envoys sent to central Asia were followed by merchants, opening the Silk Road and establishing trade links that reached as far as Europe. Production and exports of silk and ceramics were vastly increased. From India in return came tea and the new religion of Buddhism, quickly adopted and adapted by many Chinese.

Recurring throughout imperial history was the problem of the empress, or more specifically her family. Since the emperor could not think of marrying a foreign princess, or a close relation, his bride would be chosen from another important family. His in-laws were a potential threat, which became a real one if he should die when the heir to the throne was still a child. Such disputes over the succession weakened the Han dynasty and usurpers seized power. Order was restored, and the capital moved east to Luoyang in the central Yellow River valley, but the empire eventually fell apart.

Three competing states divided China; then northern and southern kingdoms rose and fell, although there were periods of comparative peace and progress. Eventually, in 581, a northern warlord succeeded in conquering the south, restoring unity under the Sui dynasty. It was to last

NAMES

The Chinese themselves have long called themselves the Han, from the first durable state to rule over most of their land. They refer to their country as Zhongguo, "The Middle Kingdom". It was foreigners who used the term China, which they may have coined on hearing of the powerful Qin (pronounced Chin) ruler and his empire. Much later, China became known for its porcelain, called "China ware", or just china.

only until 618, but in that time a start was made on a huge engineering project, linking the Yangtze and Yellow rivers by what was to become the Grand Canal. Millions of conscript workers died, and a war in Korea ended in failure and rebellion.

Tang and Song Dynasties

The general who had led the revolt became the first Tang emperor, founding a dynasty that lasted for three centuries. Their capital Xi'an, with a population of more than a million, was one of the greatest cities in the world. The Silk Road was secure, trade boomed and Chinese scholars travelled to India and beyond. Art and literature flourished; Tang 9 polychrome ceramic figures, for example, show a new originality and exuberance. When the third Tang emperor died, one of his concubines defied all precedent by marrying his successor and then ruling effectively herself as the Empress Wu.

In the later Tang era, history repeated itself. Invaders picked off distant provinces; rebels even seized the capital for a time. China again fragmented until 960 when another energetic general, Song Taizu, imposed his rule—except, ominously, in the far north where Mongol tribes had crossed the Great Wall. The development of gunpowder changed the face of war, and cities were given strong new walls, but by 1125 the Mongols occupied much of northern China.

Yuan and Ming Dynasties

Under Genghis Khan and his sons, the Mongols swept across central Asia, Persia and Russia early in the 13th century. South China's rice paddies did not suit their cavalry, so it took until 1279 to complete the conquest. For the first time in history, the whole of China was under foreign control. Kublai Khan, grandson of Genghis and founder of the Yuan dynasty, ruled from his new walled palace at Dadu, present day Beijing. Marco Polo, who claimed to have spent many years in his service, reported with admiration on the achievements of the "great khan", but he had not known what had gone before. The Mongols operated a rigid class system which antagonized the Chinese. The Yuan emperors became lazy and corrupt, and in 1368 the last of them was overthrown after an uprising in the south. Its leader declared himself the first Ming emperor and set about ensuring the future of his dynasty.

Mongol officials were brutally purged, the Great Wall was rebuilt and foreign influences were suppressed. The Ming capital, initially at Nanjing on the Yangtze, moved back to Beijing after grandiose new palaces were completed. The image of China that persists to this day, of the Forbidden City and the Great Wall, of blue porcelain and above all of mystery and "otherness", was created in the Ming era. The doors were not completely shut: the Portuguese established a trading colony at Macau, and Christian missionaries were permitted to preach, although they made few converts.

The later Ming rulers became increasingly isolated from reality, acting out arcane palace rituals surrounded by a vast, corrupt army of courtiers. In 1644, rebels seized Beijing, and the last Ming emperor hanged himself.

Qing Dynasty

Invaders from Manchuria, who had already breached the ill-defended Great Wall, now over-ran northern China and installed a new dynasty, the Qing, in Beijing, although it took another 20 years to subdue the south. Like the Mongols before them, the Manchus at first behaved as con-querors, imposing their own lan-guage, forcing their subjects to wear their hair in a pigtail and forbidding intermarriage. Soon, however, they began to ap-preciate the refinements of Chinese culture and became enthusiastic patrons of the arts.

The first four Qing emperors proved to be dynamic and effi-cient as well as long-lived: altogether, their reigns added up to 150 years. The re-sult was peace and comparative pros-perity. However, when emissaries were sent by Eu-ropean powers to seek diplo-matic contacts and especially trade, they were treated with dis-dain. China believed it-self to be the world's only civilized nation,

with nothing to gain by dealing with those it called barbarians or foreign devils. Its tea, porcelain and silk had become hugely fash-ionable in Europe, but China would only accept payment in silver, refusing to take western goods. British merchants wanted

Warrior stonily surveys the Sacred Way to the Ming Tombs.

to barter opium, cheaply produced in India. Although it was banned in China, they shipped in large quantities and paid local officials to turn a blind eye. In 1839, faced with soaring levels of opium addiction, the Chinese authorities at last took action, seizing and burning 20,000 cases of the drug in Guangzhou (Canton). In retaliation, British naval vessels bombarded it and other Chinese ports in the first Opium War. The result was inevitable: all the modern weapons were held by one side, and Guangzhou was forced to pay an extortionate "fine" or face destruction. In 1842 China had to sign the Treaty of Nanjing opening several ports to foreign trade, and ceding Hong Kong island to Britain.

Other western powers and later Japan pressed for concessions, both trade and territorial. Many times in the 19th century, war or the threat of war obliged China to sign "unequal treaties" that eroded her sovereignty. The arrogance of the foreign imperialists was often matched by the blind intransigence of the emperor's representatives. In 1860, some British envoys were tortured and killed; in revenge, British and French troops marched on Beijing and looted the exquisite Summer Palace.

The Qing hierarchy was equally unable to resist its internal enemies. The greatest of many uprisings was the Taiping Rebellion, led by a Christian zealot calling himself the Heavenly King and claiming to be the younger brother of Jesus. From small beginnings in 1850, his following grew into a vast army which controlled most of southern China, including Nanjing. But a march on Shanghai was defeated with western help, and in 1864 the Taipings were finally and bloodily crushed.

Boxer Rebellion

Defeated by Japan in a brief war, China ceded Taiwan to the victors in 1895. Domestic protest soon united under the banner of the "Boxers" (the Society of Harmonious Fists) who wanted to get rid of foreign influence, including the Christian missionaries who had gained many converts. The Empress Dowager Cixi, a former concubine who had been the power behind the throne for 40 years, saw the Boxers as a weapon to use against the hated foreigners. Many Christians were murdered, as well as the Japanese and German ministers in Beijing, and in 1900, the diplomatic quarter there was besieged. Every major world power then contributed to a relief force which routed the Boxers, while Cixi and her feeble nephew the emperor fled to Xi'an. Ever greater humiliations were heaped on China in the years that followed. Cixi at last died in 1908, the day after the emperor, who may have been poisoned on her orders. His successor Xuantong, "The Last Emperor" and later called Puyi, was only two years old.

Revolution and Republic

Many attempts had been made to overthrow Qing rule, some of them organized by the revolutionary Sun Yatsen, a doctor from Guangzhou. At last, in 1911, faced with army and peasant revolts, the moribund empire fell. Dr Sun returned from exile to proclaim the new republic, although Beijing and the north were still held by the former Qing army general, Yuan Shikai. Only when he died in 1916 was China briefly united.

With the example of the Russian revolution, a group of intellectuals and students including Mao Zedong and Zhou Enlai formed the Chinese Communist party in Shanghai in 1921. They gathered mass support, but in 1924 their Russian backers told them to support Sun Yatsen's Guomindang Nationalist regime in a campaign to crush rebellious warlords in the north.

In 1925, Sun Yatsen died, and was succeeded by his brother-in-law Chiang Kaishek (or Jiang Jieshi), an arch enemy of the Communists. Two years later, they attempted an uprising but it was quickly crushed and many of its leaders executed. Regrouping, they formed a peasant army in the south, but it came under increasing pressure from Guomindang forces. In danger of encirclement, 100,000 of them set out in 1934 on the epic Long March, trekking 9,660 km (6,000 miles), crossing 24 rivers and 18 mountain ranges, to find a secure new base in the northwest. It took a year, and only around 8,000 reached their objective. Along the route, Mao Zedong was elected party leader, a position he retained for the rest of his life.

Meanwhile in 1931 Japan had seized the Chinese province of Manchuria, installing the last Qing emperor Puyi as puppet ruler. Chiang Kaishek was more intent on fighting the Communists than the Japanese, until some of his officers arrested him and made him agree to form a united front. In spite of this, Japan launched a full-scale invasion in 1938 and rapidly occupied the north and the coastal cities. Chiang's Nationalists held out in the southwest, with American help, and Mao's Red Army in the northwest.

At the end of World War II, with their common enemy Japan defeated, Mao's Communists and Chiang's Nationalists resumed their long war against each other. The two sides rushed to occupy the vast areas vacated by the Japanese and to grab their stores of munitions. In this the Communists were, as usual, more efficient. Inflicting defeat after defeat on Chiang's forces, they also captured huge quantities of arms sent to him by the United States. By 1948, Mao's army held Manchuria and northeast China; on January 23, 1949 they took Beijing. Nanjing and Shanghai and all of southern China soon followed. Chiang fled with the remnant of his armies to Taiwan, taking China's gold reserves and many of its cultural treasures with him.

People's Republic

The victorious Communists immediately set about transforming China. Industry and business came under state control and land was distributed to the peasants. No sooner had the process begun than China was drawn into the Korean War, sending half a million "volunteers" who drove UN (mainly American) forces out of North Korea and fought them to a stalemate—a boost for morale although poisoning relations with the US for 20 years.

In the late 1950s Mao fell out with the Soviet Union. Declaring that China could go it alone he launched the Great Leap Forward, a programme of rapid industrialization and collectivization of agriculture, regardless of the human cost. The results were disastrous—production actually fell, there was famine and millions died. Only the efforts of his more pragmatic lieutenants such as premier Zhou Enlai and Deng Xiaoping kept the economy afloat.

Cultural Revolution

Facing growing opposition within his own party, in 1966 Mao mobilized student radicals to denounce "capitalist roaders" such as Deng. In no time, brigades of fanatical young Red Guards left their studies and fanned out across China, waving the Little Red Book whose real title was *Quotations from Chairman Mao*. They claimed to find "rightists", and "bourgeois revisionists" everywhere, especially in the educated and professional class. Doctors, teachers and administrators were paraded in the streets, beaten, forced into "confessions" to save their families, exiled as slave labourers on distant farms, imprisoned or killed. Soon this so-called Cultural Revolution became an attack on anything seen as "old" or foreign; temples and churches everywhere were wrecked and artistic treasures destroyed. Even Mao was eventually persuaded that his

The section of the Great Wall near the Badaling Pass is China's biggest tourist attraction.

movement had turned into a monster, but it took a massive intervention by the army to stop it.

By 1976, Mao Zedong was too ill and frail to influence events. When the more moderate Zhou Enlai died first, however, Mao's widow Jiang Qing and three collaborators ("The Gang of Four") moved to take control. But when Mao himself died on September 9, 1976, senior figures in the party and army acted fast; the Gang of Four were arrested and given long prison terms.

Deng Xiaoping gradually introduced economic reforms, permitting private business and encouraging foreign investment, while preserving the Communist party monopoly of political power. These limits to the new freedom became clear in 1989 when pro-democracy demonstrations in Beijing's Tiananmen Square were brutally crushed.

In 1997, China celebrated the return of Hong Kong and mourned the death of Deng Xiaoping, who was succeeded by Jiang Zemin, similarly committed to liberal economic policies while adhering to the principle of a disciplined one-party state. Today, under Hu Jintao, the country is in the throes of modernization, with Beijing in a frenzy of preparation for the 2008 Olympic Games. 15

On the Scene

China is just too vast to be seen in one visit, or even several. Don't try to do too much or you will finish up worn out and frustrated. A package tour has many advantages: select one with an itinerary that includes the legendary sights you've dreamed of visiting—historic and scenic—as well as a taste of the newly energized cities. This guide covers the highlights, beginning with Beijing and then moving in a geographical direction from north to south.

▶ BEIJING AND THE NORTH

Tiananmen Square, Forbidden City, Beihai Park, Temple of Heaven, Summer Palace, Ming Tombs, Great Wall, Chengde, Tianjin, Beidaihe, Dalian, Yantai, Qingdao

China's capital for most of the last seven centuries began as a small settlement in what is now the southwest district of the city. It was the centre of the northern Yan kingdom, with the name of Yanjing, from around 500 until 221 BC when China was unified by the first Qin emperor.

Genghis Khan's Mongol hordes razed it in 1215, but his grandson Kublai Khan had it rebuilt as Dadu, and made it his capital. The Ming dynasty at first preferred Nanjing but moved north early in the 15th century to the newly renamed Beijing ("Northern Capital"). Ming architects graced the city with elegant palaces, temples and parks; the Forbidden City and Temple of Heavenly Peace date from this period. The Manchu Qing emperors added to Beijing's glories, although the civil wars and foreign interventions of 1860 and 1900 caused great destruction.

Beijing today covers an area hundreds of times that of its imperial forebear. Big housing projects lie just around the corner

A sumptuous pavilion on the ramparts enclosing the Forbidden City.

from cosy back alleys; billboards promote foreign cars and TV sets rather than the party line. Entire districts are being razed to make way for facilities for the Olympic Games.

Old and New

A visit to Beijing today is exhausting but rewarding, a juxtaposition of past imperial pomp and modern dynamism. The day begins early; look out of your hotel window at dawn and you may see people doing *tai chi* or other exercises, but the broad avenues are almost empty of traffic. By 7 a.m. the great anthill has burst into activity. Waves of cyclists surge around a stream of heavy trucks, packed buses and impatient taxis in a rush hour that ebbs and flows but never really lets up for the next 12 hours.

The official figure for the population is 13 million, but that doesn't include the many who are registered somewhere else but have come to the capital to seek work. Huge in area, 16,800 sq km (6,500 sq miles), the city is mostly as flat as a table, a blessing for the cycling commuters who have enough to contend with in the winds, dust and traffic fumes. It is not a place for walking: what may look like a short walk on the map ("a couple of blocks") can turn out to be 10 km (6 miles).

The historic heart of Beijing comprised three rectangular walled cities, one within the other, and a fourth, Outer City, 8 km (5 miles) to the south. All the walls have gone apart from those shielding the innermost sanctum, the Forbidden City. A north-south axis links the main elements, from the Bell and Drum Towers in the north, then through the Forbidden City, the Gate of Heavenly Peace and Tiananmen Square.

Tiananmen Square

One of the world's largest urban spaces, with an area of 40 ha (100 acres), Tiananmen Square takes its name from the Gate of Heavenly Peace on its north side. It was greatly enlarged after the People's Republic was declared here by Mao Zedong on October 1, 1949. During the Cultural Revolution, between 1966 and 1976, as many as a million chanting Red Guards used to gather in the square, and it has become indelibly associated with the student demonstrations of 1989 and their suppression. On the western side, the Great Hall of the People (1959) in pompous Soviet style provides a venue for the leadership to address meetings of the People's Congress. Facing it on the eastern side are two museums, of Chinese history and the revolution.

Chairman Mao Zedong Memorial Hall

Near the southern end, an ugly grey box disfigures the square and interrupts the north-south vista. This is the memorial hall, quickly built (and it shows) in 1976 to contain the embalmed body of the "Great Helmsman" who ruled the People's Republic for 27 years. It is open in the morning, from Monday to Saturday, but there is often a long wait to get in. Mao's embalmed body, flag-draped in a crystal sarcophagus, is raised each day from a subterranean freezer. Silent visitors troop past it, and then through the souvenir shop (yes, even here).

Heroes' Memorial

A 60-tonne granite obelisk to the north of the Mausoleum honours those who fought against imperialism, foreign and home-grown, and in various uprisings on the way to the foundation of the People's Republic. Inscriptions on the sides reproduce Mao's calligraphy and that of Zhou Enlai, and sculpted friezes round the base depict events from the Opium Wars to the fall of the Nationalists in 1949.

Forbidden City

Officially known now as the Palace Museum, the Forbidden City (Gugong) was so called be-cause it was out of bounds to ordinary people for more than 500 years. The last emperor and his court continued to live in its palaces after the 1911 revolution, only leaving in 1924 to flee to Tianjin. Within the wall stand no fewer than 800 structures, large and small, mostly built between 1406 and 1420. Supposedly, there's a total of 9,999 rooms, an auspicious number and one short of the perfection appropriate only to the gods.

Gates

The usual entrance for visitors is through the Meridian Gate (*Wumen*) in the south wall. This massive 15th-century structure was reserved for the emperor, who made ceremonial appearances on its balcony. Beyond it is a vast courtyard, cut by a stream crossed by five marble bridges. Next in line is the Gate of Supreme Harmony (*Taihemen*), smaller and more elegant than the Meridian Gate, flanked by huge bronze lions. Like every other palace or temple building, it has a procession of small animal figures at each corner of the roof. There's always an odd number: 1, 3, 5, 7 or 9, according to the building's status, with the highest number reserved for imperial edifices. Behind the gate is an even vaster space, where the whole imperial court could assemble, as 19

From the top pavilions of Jingshan Park you can see over the rooftops of the Forbidden City.

many as 100,000 people. When the Son of Heaven entered, all but his personal guard had to kowtow—prostrate themselves face down—nine times.

Halls of Harmony

Facing this huge quadrangle is the Hall of Supreme Harmony (*Taihedian*), the largest building in the Forbidden City and the setting for imperial coronations and other great ceremonies. For centuries it was, by law, the tallest in the capital, setting a limit of 37.5 m (123 ft) on all other structures until 1911.

The line continues with the Hall of Middle (or Complete)

Harmony (*Zhonghedian*), used for receiving delegations, including foreigners, and greeting the extended imperial family.

Last in this group of palatial buildings is the Hall of Preserving Harmony (*Baohedian*), used for examinations to enter the imperial civil service, one of the few ways in which the low-born could reach a position of influence; another was to become a eunuch. On its north side is a long entrance ramp carved into a pattern of dragons and little clouds. Reserved for the emperor, carried in his litter by a party of eunuchs, it was sculpted from one huge block of marble weighing over

200 tonnes, dragged from a distant quarry by the ingenious method of sliding it over ice-covered roads in winter.

Imperial Collections

Beyond this point, to the north, the structures of the Forbidden City are lower, smaller and more densely packed. The most elaborately decorated are the emperor's bed chambers, contrasting with the spartan cells of his concubines. Many imperial possessions are on display, although here as elsewhere in China, the best pieces were taken to Taiwan by Chiang Kaishek's retreating Nationalists in 1949. Some of the western halls are used as a museum displaying bronzes, ceramics and paintings; one of the eastern palaces houses a priceless collection of clocks, mostly European, gathered together by a Qing emperor.

Imperial Garden

Near the north wall is the Imperial Garden (*Yuhuayuan*), with oddly shaped rocks, many of them brought from Lake Tai near Suzhou where they had spent thousands of years being eroded by its waters. Equally strange are the "dragon trees" with branches and twigs arched like the coils of a dragon's tail in Chinese art. Beyond the garden is the northern Gate of Martial Prowess.

Jingshan Park

Also called Coal Hill, perhaps because the imperial store of coal was kept at its base, the highest point in central Beijing stands about 90 m (almost 300 ft) above the flat surroundings at the northern edge of the Forbidden City. It is entirely artificial, built from the spoil dug out to create the city moat in the 15th century. The last Ming emperor, Chongzhen, hanged himself from a lotus tree on the hill in 1644.

At the top, where each of five separate peaks is capped by a pavilion, the view is well worth the climb. The whole layout of the Forbidden City becomes clear, as well as its relationship with the rest of Beijing.

Drum and Bell Towers

North of Coal Hill, extending the axis that runs through the Forbidden City, two massive buildings of Ming design stand clear of their neighbours. The 15th-century Drum Tower used to mark the hours of the day by the beating of a great drum; steep steps lead to the upper hall where there's a small exhibition of the history of the tower and the area. The similar Bell Tower, rebuilt after an 18th century fire, still has the huge bell that used to wake the city at 5 a.m.

Many princes and courtiers owned palaces in this area. A few have been adapted for use as schools and clinics, but one of the best, Prince Gong's Palace (*Gongwangfu*), has been preserved and restored. The Beijing Opera holds performances in a small theatre in its gardens.

Hutong District

Looking down from the Drum Tower you'll have seen a labyrinth of narrow streets, called *hutong*, lined by old courtyard houses. In the traditional style, four low buildings (sometimes housing different families) surrounded an open quadrangle, but pressure on space means that most have been partly filled in by more construction. A wall across the inside of the gateway of each compound, intended to keep evil spirits out, blocks the view from the street. If you take an organized tour by trishaw, you can see inside some of the houses and meet the residents. In spite of the cramped conditions, they much prefer to live here than in remote suburbs with a long commute. Even so, until recently there were plans to bulldoze the remaining *hutong* districts; now, as a tourist attraction, they may survive.

Beihai Park

Below Coal Hill to the west, Beihai Park and its lake date from the 12th century. This was the site of Kublai Khan's 13th-century palace, where Marco Polo is said to have stayed as his guest. Now it's a favourite place for young couples to stroll or rent a rowing boat. The Bridge of Eternal Peace leads to an island, with a Tibetan-style tower, the White Dagoba, built in 1651 to mark a visit by the Dalai Lama. At the north end of the lake, the Ming Dynasty Nine Dragon Wall has a ceramic-tile picture of dragons playing with pearls amid a stormy sea.

Temple of Heaven

South of the Forbidden City, an equally large area was set aside solely for religious ceremonies and used on fewer than ten days of the year. With an assembly of buildings that represent the zenith of Ming architecture, this was where the emperor came to pray and make sacrifices for a good harvest, and the best approach is the one his procession took, through the south entrance. Other gates are on the north and west sides. Once inside, you first come to a square compound (the earth), enclosing a round altar, consisting of three terraces of marble. A stone at the centre of the upper terrace has nine stones around it; the next ring has 18 and so on to 81. Multiples of 3, 5, 7 and especially 9 were regarded as auspicious, and are still seen as lucky to this day; hotels like to have 999 in their telephone numbers. From the centre of the altar, the emperor would communicate directly with the sky (heaven). The green-tiled structure to the south of the altar is the oven where a sacrificial ox was incinerated.

Imperial Vault of Heaven

North of the round altar is a circular wall; inside is a circular building with a conical roof, not at the centre but offset. Ritual objects used to be stored here. Echoes round the enclosing wall are supposed to let you speak to someone on the opposite side of the compound, but there's usually far too much noise from the crowds.

Hall of Prayer for a Good Harvest

A long path, formerly reserved for the emperor, leads to the tallest, most significant and beautiful building in the Temple of Heaven complex. Here on the 15th day of the first lunar month (usually in February or March), the emperor made sacrificial offerings. Circular with a conical, three-level pagoda roof, the hall is beautifully proportioned but sadly shabby, although it is just a replica of the 16th-century Ming original. That was destroyed by fire, caused by lightning in 1889. The tiles have now lost their deep blue lustre, just as the Forbidden City's tiles have lost most of the golden-yellow which once dazzled the eyes.

The East Hall of the compound houses a collection of traditional musical instruments; the West Hall, some porcelain and bronzes. At the western entrance to the Temple of Heaven, the Hall of Abstinence was where the emperor fasted and meditated before the rituals.

Summer Palace

Wooded hills and a lake, 16 km (10 miles) northwest of the Forbidden City, are the setting of the Summer Palace (Yiheyuan) built for Empress Cixi in the 1880s. "Palace" scarcely describes the 280 ha (700 acres) of landscaped park, with temples and pavilions, a theatre, bridges and fountains. It is said that funds intended to modernize the Chinese navy were used to create this earthly paradise, thus contributing to defeat by the Japanese. If so, the elaborate two-deck marble boat on Kunming Lake was an especial folly. Another striking feature is a covered walkway, curving for over 700 m (800 yd) and painted with scenes of southern China.

Old Summer Palace

Little was left of the glory of the previous summer retreat of the Qing emperors after British and French troops looted and then

BEIJING ZOO

In the northwestern area of the city, 12 km (7 miles) from the centre, the zoo's main attraction for foreign visitors is its handful of pandas. Endangered in the wild, here they lie around in comparative comfort, chewing their special bamboo shoots. The rest of the inmates suffer in cramped cages; this zoo has not adopted modern, open-plan methods.

burned it in 1860. The looting was permitted, and the burning ordered, by their leader the Earl of Elgin, in revenge for the torture and murder of several of his staff. They had been trying to force the imperial authorities into trade negotiations, but their seizure by the Chinese triggered a march on Beijing by the western armies. The old palace (*Yuanmingyuan*) had been a wonder of the world, a huge park with lakes, jewelled pavilions, exotic fish and animals. Its strange half-Chinese, half-baroque mansions were designed in the 18th century for Emperor Qianlong with the help of Jesuit missionaries.

After its destruction, the Empress Cixi abandoned the ruins and had the present Summer Palace built about 5 km (3 miles) to the west. A few stones were

reassembled into monuments, with signs condemning imperialist aggression; otherwise the vast park was almost forgotten. Now the maze has been restored, there's a dinosaur park and a Garden History Exhibition Hall.

Ming Tombs

At about the time the Ming rulers moved north from Nanjing to Beijing, the third Ming emperor Yongle ordered a search for a suitable site for his tomb. In 1407 he chose the Shisanling valley, 40 km (25 miles) northwest of Beijing, where he and 11 of his 12 successors were to be buried.

A 16th-century marble gateway marks the beginning of the Sacred Way leading to the tombs. Then comes a triple-arched gate; the central arch was only used when an emperor's body was brought for interment. Beyond the gate, the route is lined by larger-than-life statues of men and animals, real and mythical, carved in stone in the 15th century.

Only two of the tombs are open to visitors. The largest and oldest, known as Changling, is that of Yongle himself. A succession of courtyards, marble ter-

The imperial family spent their holidays in the cool surroundings of the Summer Palace.

races and palatial buildings centres on the great Hall of Eminent Favours, one of the largest wooden buildings in China.

Dingling, the tomb of Wanli (emperor from 1573 to 1620) is the only one to have been fully excavated. It is said that 30,000 workers laboured for six years to create this underground palace. Some of the original jewels, robes, regalia and artefacts are on display at the site.

On the way to the most popular part of the Great Wall, the Ming Tombs can be packed with people, and the authorities have added other attractions in the area to entice even more. Escape the crowds by walking to some of the 11 unrestored and unopened tombs, neglected but still beautiful and surrounded by vestiges of their formal gardens.

The Great Wall

From the shores of the Yellow Sea to the Gobi Desert, the world's most colossal construction snakes through barren hills and along mountain ridges for over 5,000 km (more than 3,000 miles), justifying the Chinese name, the Wall of Ten Thousand Li (one *li* being equivalent to 500 m). It's not just a single fortification, but a whole system. In places it divides into two or more lines, with many outlying and unconnected sections.

Its origins date from 2500 years ago, when warring states began to build walls between their territories. The ruthless Qin emperor who united most of China by 221 BC then decreed that various sections marking the northern boundary of his empire should be joined up. Huge numbers of people were conscripted for the work; the forced labour of millions became the method of construction through the ensuing centuries, whenever successive dynasties perceived a threat from the barbarians to the north.

At times, the Wall became redundant, when the empire became so strong that it expanded far beyond it. But the Ming emperors felt especially threatened by the Manchus on the northern border, and massively strengthened it. To no avail; the Manchus invaded, overthrew them and established the Qing dynasty. Unlike their predecessors, the Qing emperors declined to repair the Wall, perhaps reasoning that it hadn't been effective against *them*. Whole sections were looted for building material or crumbled into ruins.

Badaling Pass

The most accessible, and most visited, part of the Wall is at Badaling, 70 km (44 miles) northwest of Beijing. This was the first section to be restored under the People's Republic and opened for organized tourism in the 1950s. It has spawned a vast encampment of souvenir stands and restaurants. On the Wall itself, although the roadway along the top is a full 6 m (20 ft) wide, the crowds are at times so great that it's hard to make progress. If you have time to persist, keep walking, and you will eventually leave the hordes behind. About one kilometre (half a mile) north of the entry point, the heavily restored section ends, and only the romantic vestiges of the Great Wall march away into the lonely distance.

Mutianyu

Less crowded than Badaling, a short section of the Wall in the rolling hills about 90 km (56 miles) northeast of Beijing has been restored, with its imposing guard towers. A cable car offers an alternative to the steep flights of steps up from the entrance. Up on the Wall itself, if you are prepared to walk and climb more steps, you can get to places that the tour groups don't reach.

Jinshanling Pass

The road from Beijing to the old imperial mountain retreat of Chengde intersects the Great Wall at Jinshanling, about 150 km (93 miles) from the capital. A short drive and a walk up a steep track and you're at the Wall itself. In this sector, partially restored, it snakes across a wild, rugged landscape, disappearing into the misty distance with no sign of cultivation or any habitation in sight. Few visitors come this far from Beijing, so with luck, you'll have the experience of walking (or climbing—there are countless steps) the Wall in comparative solitude. You won't be completely alone, because local Mongolian people stationed near the starting point attach themselves to visitors as self-appointed assistants, ready to help you up steps or on rough sections, whether you need it or not. If you walk quickly enough, you will leave them behind, but they'll wait for your return and try to sell you a T-shirt or other souvenir.

Chengde

Set in a river valley amid the Yunshan mountains 250 km (155 miles) northeast of Beijing in Hebei province, Chengde (formerly Jehol) was the summer retreat of the Qing emperors during the four hottest months of the year, from June to September. Travelling in litters or on horseback, the imperial party took only a week to make the journey. Today it's a 4-hour drive, not including a stop at the Great Wall on the way. Approaching Chengde, the road descends into 27

Say cheese! Sightseers fit into the picture at Chengde.

a long valley, where large parts of the flat valley floor have been covered in plastic greenhouses, growing early salad crops and vegetables for the cities to the south. Mules pull ploughs across the fields, and the rocky mountain slopes have been planted with trees in a huge reafforestation scheme.

The Qing dynasty emperor who began the habit of spending summers in Chengde was Kangxi (1662–1722), who was drawn to it by the good hunting and cool climate. He probably also felt an affinity with the rugged scenery, reminiscent of the northern home of his Manchu forbears. There

was a political element too; in building here the rulers of China could display their power to the Mongol tribes of the region, north of the Great Wall.

Following the policy of keeping the non-Chinese minorities who lived on the periphery of the huge empire happy, or at least overawed, the Qing emperors organized gatherings of their leaders at Chengde. As a gesture of hospitality and a display of munificence, temples were built in the styles of their homelands, notably small versions of Tibetan Buddhist lamaseries. At one time there were twelve, but fire and neglect took their toll and only eight survive, scattered in the hills around Chengde. The town itself is quite nondescript, apart from its backdrop of mountains and the river running through it.

Imperial Palace and Park

On the northern edge of town, a wall 10 km (6 miles) long surrounds the imperial domain. Just inside the main gate, the palace was built early in the 18th century. In contrast to the magnificence of the Forbidden City, it is remarkably restrained. Only one or two storeys high, with minimal decoration, it gives an impression of modest elegance—even the emperor's chambers are quite small. Several of the rooms have been restored and equipped with Qing dynasty furniture; others house fine examples of porcelain, jade and calligraphy.

More palaces and pavilions are dotted around the park, landscaped to resemble beauty spots of southern China, with lakes and pagodas, next to a tamed version of the mountainous north.

Putuozongsheng Temple

High on a hillside north of the imperial domain, Putuozongsheng (Potaraka Doctrine) is the biggest of the temples. It was built from 1767–71, to look like the Potala Palace in Lhasa, and although smaller than the original, it is still imposing. Several

CONTENT WITH HIS LOT

The first British diplomatic mission to the imperial court, led by Lord Macartney, had hoped to see the emperor in Beijing, but had to make the additional journey to Chengde, in September 1793. The emperor, Qianlong (1736–95), received Macartney but brushed aside his proposals of a treaty or trade, saying that China needed no allies or foreign goods: "We already possess everything".

flights of steep steps lead to the main building, whose dour walls conceal a highly decorated temple with a golden roof. And in this case, it really is golden; the copper tiles are covered with an estimated one tonne of gold. On the more accessible lower parts of the roof, you can see where Japanese soldiers who occupied Chengde from 1931 to 1945 scraped some of it off.

Puning Temple

The Temple of Universal Tranquillity (1755), northeast of the park, is notable for a great effigy of Guanyin, the Goddess of Mercy (sometimes identified with the feminine aspect of Buddha). Standing 22.3 m (73 ft) high, it is said to be the biggest wooden 29 statue in the world, made of many types of wood. The walls of the chamber have niches for over 10,000 small Buddha figures (some have been lost). After a long absence, shaven-headed monks are back at the temple, pursuing their devotions and organizing the sale of souvenirs.

Pule Temple

To the east of the park, the Temple of Universal Happiness dates from 1766, and like all the outer temples, it faces the imperial palace. The main hall recalls the Temple of Heaven in Beijing, but the images within depict some of the stranger interpretations of Buddhist enlightenment, four-faced figures copulating and sexual congress between a woman and a bull.

Hammer Peak

Not far from Pule, Bangchuishan or Sledgehammer Rock sticks up like a huge thumb on the eastern horizon. The easy way to reach it is by a 20-minute ride on a chairlift, suspended over hills and valleys planted with apple and almond orchards, a sea of pale pink blossom in spring. The rock, 52 m (171 ft) high, is a crumbling mass of aggregate, a sedimentary rock like natural concrete, but legend recounts that a dragon stuck it there to plug a hole which was letting the sea pour out.

Tianjin

North China's biggest industrial city grew up as the port for Beijing, 120 km (75 miles) inland. Ocean-going ships used to dock in the centre of Tianjin, but the Hai river silted up, and ships became much bigger. The port area is now 50 km (30 miles) downstream at Tanggu, where the Hai meets the Bohai Gulf.

Britain and France gained trading and residence rights after their warships bombarded the coastal forts in the war of 1856–58. They were later joined by Japan, Russia, Italy and other European nations, and some of the mansions, schools and barracks they built can still be seen in the former foreign concessions along the river in the heart of the old city. A landmark on the north bank is the French-built cathedral (1903–04); it replaced one burned down in the Boxer Rising. Otherwise, there are few historic buildings; a severe earthquake devastated the neighbouring city of Tangshan in 1976 and badly damaged Tianjin as well. Many visitors head for the antiques market west of the city centre; it's reckoned to be a more promising hunting ground than the capital.

Beidaihe

Diplomats and missionaries living in Tianjin and Beijing in the 1890s first discovered the attrac-

Don't miss the chance to brush up your calligraphic skills.

tions of the beaches on Bohai Gulf. Beidaihe was the first resort, where foreigners built seaside villas and summer houses. After the Communist takeover, it became popular with party bosses, who had their own segregated beach. Senior officials still come to Beidaihe, but most visitors are ordinary people from Beijing, or favoured workers who can stay in one of the many sanatoria.

Dalian

Near the southern tip of Liaodong Peninsula, Dalian's strategic position explains its chequered history and importance today. With its neighbour, Lushun (formerly Port Arthur), it commands the approach to Tianjin. To the east lie North and South Korea. Its ice-free port serves heavily industrialized northeastern China, historically known as Manchuria.

Russia occupied Port Arthur at the end of the 19th century and made it a naval base. A nearby fishing village was expanded as the commercial port of Dalny ("far away"). Japan gained them both after defeating Russia in the brief war between them in 1905. Dalny (Dairen to the Japanese, Dalian today) became the terminus of the Manchuria Railway, and is still an important rail 31 centre. Russia (by this time the Soviet Union) was back at the end of World War II, while Mao's Communists controlled the region. Relations between them were often strained, and the Russians finally left in 1955.

In recent years Dalian has been a magnet for foreign investment, in the chemical, steel, electronics and motor industries, shipbuilding and the port installations. New international hotels have sprung up, and people are as fashionably dressed as in Shanghai or even Hong Kong. But you can still find old Japanese and Russian buildings amid the modern construction: the spacious centre (to a Tsarist Russian plan), 1930s office blocks, a former Russian Orthodox church, even a mock-Tudor mansion. Hemmed in by hill and the sea, Dalian still has a more open feeling than most Chinese cities, with easy access to pleasant beaches.

The Harbour

The port is busy year-round with container ships and freighters from half the world's trading nations, plus the occasional cruise ship on a voyage along the coast of China. Near the gate to the dock area, the Dalian International Seamen's Club is a seven-storey building with many facilities, not only for their crews but other foreign visitors too. A ground-level shop sells many basic necessities as well as postcards and souvenirs. A wider range of craft goods is available at the nearby Friendship department store.

City Centre

Excursion buses make the lengthy circuit of the main square, which is in fact a huge circle. Enormous official buildings face this great plaza, called Zhongshan Square in honour of Dr Sun Yatsen. Also in the city centre, the Museum of Natural History has exhibits on the flora and fauna of the region, especially marine life, and its minerals, the basis of major industries. Tours of Dalian may include the glass works, which makes glass pictures as well as utilitarian products, and the shell-carving factory, where hundreds of workers turn seashell fragments into three-dimensional tableaux, versions of Chinese paintings.

A notable feature of Dalian is its underground city—not a shopping mall or subway but built as a civil defence measure in the 1970s, for use in the event of an air raid.

Beaches and Countryside

Tourists come from other parts of China to enjoy Dalian's beaches and seafood restaurants. The best beaches are to the south of the city, notably Laohutan or Tiger Beach Park, an amusement park with a sandy shoreline set among pine trees. It's commercial and tends to be crowded, but other smaller coves are quieter. At low tide, the local shellfish hunters scour the rocks and seaweed collectors find the tastiest varieties. Seaweed is also gathered on an industrial scale; an overhead conveyor system hauls it ashore, not only for eating but for extracting alginates (jelling agents) and as fertilizer. The rolling hills round Dalian grow soybeans, sorghum and some of China's best apples.

Yantai

On the north coast of the Shandong peninsula, Yantai (formerly Chefoo) stands at the entrance to the Bohai Gulf, guarding the approaches to Tianjin—and thus Beijing. Its name, meaning Smoke Tower, recalls its role as a lookout post; the sentries set fire to wolf dung to send smoke signals if hostile ships were sighted. British and French forces occupied the town in 1860, and it became a treaty port. German development of Qingdao to the south, especially the railway which reached it in 1904, put Yantai in the shade, until the US Pacific fleet began to use it as a base in the 1920s. The Communist government earmarked it for industrialization and joined it to the railway in the 1950s. Today it's a major fishing port.

Apart from the pockets of industry, Shandong has always been a rich agricultural region, with apple and cherry orchards, as well as vineyards producing some of China's better wines and brandies.

City Sights

Yantai's harbour is usually busy with cargo ships and deep-sea trawlers, rusty and storm-battered. A couple of sandy beaches east of the port attract summer sunbathers. Inland, the city is surrounded by rolling hills; the best view of it is from Yuhuang Peak, with an old temple as landmark.

Yantai Museum displays local archaeological finds and Ming porcelain, but the real highlights are the buildings that house them. One is a former merchants' hall, with superb stone and wood carvings; another is the ornate and beautiful Temple to the Sea Goddess in Song dynasty style, one of the finest of its kind to survive in China.

Qingdao

A major port and industrial city may not sound like an enticing place for a visit, but Qingdao has some surprises and a unique history. Its beaches of fine white sand, right next to the city, make Qingdao one of China's most

33

popular seaside resorts; a profusion of parks and gardens adds to the relaxed atmosphere. And if the old centre around the railway station reminds you of Germany, that's because it was German-built.

Germany had long nursed ambitions of establishing a naval and trading base on the Chinese coast. In 1897, two German priests were killed in Shandong province, and on the pretext of restoring public safety, German forces seized the small port of Qingdao. China was compelled to sign a 99-year lease, granting Germany wide-ranging rights in the region. The occupiers set about building docks and piers, a modern town and a railway to Jinan, the capital of Shandong. Industries were set up including a brewery, which still exists, producing the best-known brand of beer in China, Tsingtao (the city's old name).

When World War I erupted in Europe in 1914, Japan joined in against Germany, mainly to grab the Kaiser's Chinese beachhead. After the war was over, to the fury of the Chinese authorities, the Treaty of Versailles high-handedly transferred the balance of Germany's 99-year lease to Japan. China did regain Shandong, including Qingdao, in 1922, although the Japanese occupied it again from 1938 to

A few members of the older generation still wear a "Mao" costume.

1945. After the Communist victory in 1949, it became the focus of rapid expansion; many German villas were turned into workers' sanatoria.

Harbours and Beaches

The modern port is on the north side of the city, and the southern shore is the focus of the holiday area, with souvenir stalls, ice-cream stands and professional photographers drumming up business among the crowds of visitors. The pier where German ships used to tie up, now lengthened to 440 m (480 yd), is a popular promenade, and an octagonal pavilion at the end exhibits Shandong arts and crafts. Back on shore, an aquarium houses the varied local sealife in 60 big glass tanks, and the nearby Marine Products Museum displays the goods derived from the sea. Between the two are pools with resident seals, sealions and turtles. Offshore, you may see the sailing dinghies of Qingdao's yacht club, the first of its kind in China.

Treat yourself to a tour in one of the open-top limousines, highly unusual for China. East of the old harbour, the seafront villas grow more impressive, culminating in the Granite Castle, a tall stone mansion with a commanding view. Inland, Zhongshan Park is the city's biggest, with lush vegetation and the local zoo. Xin-

---

BEER-TASTING

Another German legacy is the celebrated Tsingtao beer, sent in its sturdy green bottles, and nowadays cans, to all parts of China. The century-old vats have been replaced by modern equipment (likewise German-made), but the process would still be approved by the founders. Tours can be arranged with, of course, a tasting.

---

hao Hill Park near the centre is the site of a fine old mansion turned into a hotel, and has the best views, unless you go to the top of Qingdao's TV tower. Visible to the west are the twin spires of the Catholic Church, still active, as is a Protestant church not far away.

Laoshan

A mountainous area about 40 km (25 miles) east of Qingdao, Laoshan is famous for its waterfalls, woods and caves. Its well-known mineral water is bottled at the source; the same water goes to make Tsingtao beer, and grapes grown on the lower slopes are used for the well-known Huadong white wines. A cable car takes you part-way up the mountain; then you have to hike to the 1133-m (3720-ft) summit.

35

XI'AN AND THE SILK ROAD

Walled City, Outside the Walls,
Tomb of Qin Shihuang, Terracotta Warriors,
Xianyang, Famen Temple, Silk Road

Shaanxi in central China is one of the more go-ahead provinces of the mainly impoverished interior, producing everything from apples to aircraft. Its capital, Xi'an, 880 km (550 miles) southwest of Beijing, was the capital of China during the glorious golden age of the Tang dynasty (618–907), when it was known as Chang'an. Even in decline it remained significant as the eastern end of the ancient Silk Road, and was given strong

new walls in the Ming period. The Empress Dowager Cixi fled to Xi'an after the Boxer rising, and Chiang Kaishek was briefly arrested near the city in 1936 in the strange Xi'an incident.

It had long been known as the centre of a rich archaeological region. Then the news broke in 1974 of the sensational discovery of thousands of pottery figures, more than lifesize, dating from the Qin empire, 2200 years ago. Labelled the "Ter-racotta Warriors",

this buried army was instantly and rightly catapulted on to the short list of wonders of the world. Ever-increasing numbers of visitors flocked to Xi'an; international hotels sprang up to house them and a fine new airport was built.

The Walled City

The walls you see today date from early in the Ming dynasty, around 1370; they were strengthened and faced with brick two centuries later. Rectangular in plan, they are aligned north-south and east-west, and although the city looks compact on a map, the walls are more than 12 km (8 miles) in circumference. Each side has one main gate, built like a fortress with a tower and large enclosed compound. Traditional greeting and farewell ceremonies are staged for tourists at the North

Gate. It's worth climbing to the top of the wall, and possible to walk along it in places, especially the eastern and southern sections, descending to ground level at the gates and several other points where the walls have been pierced in modern times to ease the flow of traffic.

Towers

The Ming Bell Tower, near the intersection of the main streets, is a great wooden structure with a triple-eaved roof, all built without a single nail. A 16th-century bell weighing two tonnes still hangs ready for use. The nearby Drum Tower, not quite as prominent, signalled the curfew at night and the opening of the gates in the

Monument in Xi'an recalls the city's significance as the beginning of the Silk Road.

morning; anyone caught outside between those hours had to stay there.

Muslim Quarter

To the west of the Drum Tower are narrow streets and alleys lined by low wooden houses, tiny shops and stalls, like a Middle Eastern bazaar. The resemblance is no coincidence—this is the Muslim Quarter, where some 25,000 people of the Hui minority live. They are the descendants of Arab mercenary soldiers and traders who used the Silk Road, settled in Xi'an and intermarried with the local people. On the northern edge of the quarter, the Great Mosque where they worship was founded in the 8th century. It looks less like a mosque than a collection of Chinese pavilions and gateways, set in an ornamental garden; even the carpeted prayer hall is lit by typically Chinese lanterns. If it were not for the inscriptions in Arabic writing, the mode of worship and the coming and going at the bathhouse, it could be mistaken for a Buddhist temple.

Shaanxi Provincial Museum

Close to the South Gate, the museum occupies a former Confucian temple. Most of its galleries are taken up by the Forest of Steles, a library comprising more than 2000 standing stone slabs and tablets. Many date from the Tang dynasty, when they were created to set in stone, literally, the most important Confucian texts and historical records. Some of them include maps: one of Chang'an, the Tang name for the city, shows that it covered a much greater area than today.

Outside the Walls

A short distance beyond the south gate, the Small Wild Goose Pagoda dates from the late 7th century. It is part of a still-active Buddhist Jianfu temple; every morning the monks toll a huge iron bell, which resounds over a large part of the city. The jagged shape of the top resulted from an earthquake that broke off two of its 15 storeys.

The brick and wood Big Wild Goose Pagoda, 3 km (2 miles) to the southeast, is part of the biggest temple in Xi'an. Built in the 7th century to house precious Buddhist texts brought from India, it has been rebuilt several times; the original had only five storeys. Climb to the top, 60 m (200 ft) up, for a great view. On the east side of the temple is a modern museum devoted entirely to Tang Dynasty Arts.

Shaanxi History Museum

In a modern building between the Big and Small Wild Goose pagodas, this museum has the best general collection of the region's archaeology from all eras, well displayed in chronological order and labelled in English as well as Chinese. Among the highlights are frescoes removed from Tang dynasty tombs showing dances and hunting scenes, magnificent Tang ceramics, jewellery and costumes.

Banpo Stone Age Village

About 8 km (5 miles) east of Xi'an, Banpo Village was unearthed by chance in the 1950s. Construction workers alerted archaeologists who discovered a Neolithic settlement dating from around 4000 BC, with the foundations of round and square houses, barns and kilns, as well as the decorated pottery that was made in them. The adjoining burial ground yielded skeletons and grave goods: jade and bone ornaments and ceramic bowls, some of them on show in the site museum. The women's graves contained far more than the men's, leading to the theory that this was a matriarchal society. A roof covers the excavations, which you can view from walkways.

Tomb of Qin Shihuang

When he came to the throne of the Qin kingdom in 246 BC, Qin Shihuang was only 13 years old, but as was the custom, work started on his mausoleum right away. As his power grew—he was to be the first emperor of a unified Chinese state—so did the plans become ever more grandiose. By the time of his death in 210 BC, a whole subterranean city had been built, with another city on the surface, enclosed by inner and outer walls, roughly 6 km (4 miles) long and 9 km (6 miles) across. According to a Han dynasty historian, writing a century later, there were underground lakes of mercury, and vast quantities of gold and jewels. When the emperor was buried, all his concubines who had no children were entombed along with him, and an artificial hill 115 m (378 ft) high was built over the spot.

Today, the hill is the only visible sign, standing out in the plain about 32 km (20 miles) east of Xi'an. It has been eroded down to a height of about 76 m (250 ft). Stone steps lead to the top, but there is little to see. Protected by the respect accorded to the dead, the tomb itself has never been excavated, and archaeologists have their hands full with discoveries round its perimeter. Intriguingly, samples taken by drilling into the mausoleum show very high levels of mercury compounds, giving credence to the old accounts.

The Terracotta Warriors

In the spring of 1974, some peasants were digging a well not far to the east of the Qin emperor's tomb. They found no water, but broken pieces of terracotta figures depicting soldiers and horses, and the remains of ancient bronze weapons. What they had stumbled on was part of a great pottery army, designed to accompany the emperor into the afterlife. Within two years, three huge pits had been uncovered, containing more than 7,000 figures of warriors, just over lifesize, with hundreds of horses, generally in lines of four, interspersed among them. The chariots that they were pulling were made of wood and have long since rotted or burned away, although impressions of them can be seen in the earth.

Historians suggest that Qin Shihuang might originally have wanted his real imperial guard to be buried with him, but realised their morale and perhaps loyalty would suffer when they heard of the plan. The replicas were placed in battle order in pits about 5 m (16 ft) deep. Wooden pillars supported a wooden roof, covered with woven mats, clay and earth. There is evidence of fire damage, probably soon after the pits were closed. (Some historians believe that they were looted and burned when the Qin dynasty was overthrown in 206 BC.) Then, over the centuries the remaining wood rotted, the roof

collapsed and mud washed in to fill the pits.

The warriors were not made in one piece, but assembled from a solid lower half, a hollow torso and separate head. Although the bodies were mass-produced, the heads are all subtly different, with distinctive facial features; it has even been suggested that some are actual portraits. When they were discovered, all the figures had been broken into at least ten fragments, often many more, and these were embedded in dried mud which had set almost as hard and looked much the same as the terracotta. The problem for the excavators was daunting.

The Pits

Enormous sheds like aircraft hangars have been built to protect the treasures. Visitors view them from raised walkways, and the first sight of the ranks of warriors is truly breathtaking.

Pit No 1, the largest, measures 210 m (230 yd) by 62 m (68 yd) and contains an estimated 7,000 figures. More than 1,000 have been uncovered and reassembled, but the archaeologists are now taking their time. The techniques used in the early stages did not preserve the original thin layer of pigment that covered the figures and must have made the army a colourful sight. And exposure to air and pollution—not least the

damp breath of thousands of visitors each day —has begun to cause moulds to grow.

Pit No 2, on the northeast side of No 1, is T-shaped, 124 m (135 yd) across and 98 m (107 yd) long. It holds about 1500 warriors, many of them being archers, standing or kneeling, or cavalrymen with horses. The degree of damage is much greater than in No 1, and excavation is less far advanced.

Pit No 3, U-shaped and much smaller than the others, seems to represent the army's headquarters, with 68 figures of important-looking officers in rows facing each other, similar to a guard of honour.

Museum

When they were placed in the vaults, all the warriors were equipped with bows and arrows, swords and spears made of bronze and wood. Thousands of the bronze weapons have survived, and some are on display. So are two bronze chariots, beautifully illuminated, in a museum near Pit No 2. The first is a war chariot, the second is the emperor's own; both are drawn by four bronze horses and driven by a bronze charioteer. Made to roughly half lifesize, these are marvels of intricate detail; each of the sturdy little horses has its own individual character, and every bolt and strap of the harness is so clearly defined it would be easy to replicate them today. Like the warriors, they were painted in a variety of bright colours; traces are still visible.

Huaqing Hot Springs

Excursions to the Army of Terracotta Warriors usually make a stop at the Huaqing Hot Springs, a former imperial retreat with centuries of historical significance. The mineral waters welling out of Black Horse Mountain at a pleasant 43°C (109°F) attracted royal visitors since the 8th century BC. A complex of gardens, pavilions and pools grew up, and Qin, Han and Tang dynasty rulers spent time there relaxing with their concubines.

A highlight for Chinese tourists is the mosaic-lined oval tub in which Yang Guifei, concubine of the Tang emperor Xuan Zong, used to bathe. The visitors know the classical poems that recount her fate. To pacify mutinous courtiers and generals who said the emperor was spending too much time with her and neglecting affairs of state, Xuan Zong is said to have ordered her death, and then abdicated.

Much more recently, other rebellious generals imprisoned the Nationalist leader Chaing Kaishek in 1936, until he agreed to stop trying to crush Mao Zedong's Communists and join them in fighting the Japanese who were sweeping across north China.

Xianyang

You would never guess that the industrial city of Xianyang, 24 km (15 miles) northwest of Xi'an, was the capital of the Qin Empire 22 centuries ago. The countryside around is dotted with burial mounds dating from the later Han dynasty; you will see some of them on the way from Xi'an Airport, north of Xianyang. Some have been excavated, and Xianyang Museum has a splendid terracotta army—in miniature. The figures of the soldiers, 2000 of them, are only about 50 cm (20 in) tall. They were discovered in the 1960s.

Tang Tombs

To the northwest, some 60 km (37 miles) from Xianyang, there is an important group of royal tombs from the Tang dynasty. Qian Ling is the mausoleum of the third Tang emperor, Gao Zong, and his scheming widow, the former concubine Wu Zetian, who managed to have herself proclaimed empress in her own right after his death in 683. She was the only woman to have achieved this in ancient China. The tomb remains unexcavated, but the Royal Way is impressive, lined with statues of winged horses, mythical birds and envoys from vassal states, now sadly headless.

Famen Temple

Located 120 km (75 miles) west of Xi'an, Famen was a famous Buddhist temple, built to house four sacred bones of a finger of Buddha, the gift of Emperor Ashoka of India in the 3rd century BC. It became an important place of pilgrimage, especially during the Tang era. In later centuries, earthquakes and floods damaged the site; the underground vault containing the relics was buried and largely forgotten. Not until the 1980s, during a restoration project, was the chamber rediscovered—with the fingerbones still in their elaborate multiple caskets. Together with them was a wonderful collection of Tang dynasty treasures—stone tablet Buddhist scriptures, coins, objects in gold and silver—now displayed in a museum at the site.

The Silk Road

For centuries, the Silk Road was the thread which connected East and West, a hazardous route across the deserts of northwest China to central Asia, Persia and the Middle East. As well as trade, it carried ideas: art forms, inventions and even religions made their way in both directions. Until the 2nd century BC, there was no link; China and the rest of the world lived in mutual ignorance. Then, from Chang'an, their capital (now Xi'an), the Han emperors began to send emissaries beyond their western borders, at first to buy some of the magnificent horses bred by the tribes who lived there. The traders who followed reached Persia, where they found a ready market for their silk. Local merchants sent it further west, to the Mediterranean lands of the Roman empire, and scored an instant success. The Romans had an insatiable appetite for luxuries and plenty of gold to pay for them; China had a monopoly in silk, hitherto unobtainable in the west where people still had no idea how the thread was produced.

The distances involved were vast, with forbidding deserts and high mountain passes to cross. It is 3,000 km (1,800 miles) from Xi'an to Kashgar, all within Chinese territory. When China was strong, imperial power reached this far west, protecting travellers from bandits and providing garrisons for the oases along the route. When it was in decline, only large, well-defended caravans dared to make the journey. In times of war, traffic practically ceased.

The Silk Road experienced a renaissance in the 13th century

after the Mongols conquered its entire length and imposed order for almost a hundred years. Marco Polo's tales of his travels date from this period. But with the fall of the Mongol Yuan dynasty, the road again became too dangerous; sea routes eventually took over its role.

Today, adventure tourism has brought new travellers to the dusty oasis towns of the Silk Road, but journeys that used to take months are covered in days by train and bus, and mere hours by plane.

Dunhuang

True desert begins at Dunhuang, 1,200 km (750 miles) west of Xi'an; great sand dunes loom close to the edge of town. Today's visitors come to see the unique Mogao Caves, a 30-minute drive to the south. Here, in the 4th century AD, the first Buddhist temples in China were hewn out of the steep cliffs, and decorated with a wonderful variety of wall-paintings and carvings, including Tang dynasty Buddha statues 33 m (110 ft) high. Work continued on and off for the next 1,000 years, but when the Silk Road fell out of use, the caves were sealed up and abandoned. They were rediscovered in 1900 by a Buddhist monk.

Almost 500 caves have been recorded, and about 30 are open to visitors. In the earliest, the art shows strong Indian influences; later styles are closer to Tibetan. The colours are miraculously preserved, and to protect them the caves are unlit and photography is banned. Guides carry torches (flashlights); it's a good idea to do the same.

Urumqi

West of Dunhuang, travellers on the Silk Road left the protection of the Great Wall. The route split into northern and southern routes, the northern branch heading for Urumqi. Up to the 1960s this was a poor backwater. Now it is a modern concrete city with a population of 1.2 million, the capital of the Xinjiang Uighur Autonomous Region which covers one-sixth of the land area of China. About a dozen minority ethnic groups make up most of the region's 18 million people; half are Uighurs, Muslims of central Asian origin.

Turpan

In contrast to Urumqi's highrises and fashion boutiques, Turpan (Turfan), two hours' drive away, is a traditional oasis where there are more donkey carts than cars. Grapes are its main product, fresh or as raisins, and the whole town seems to be curtained in vines. Tours of the area take in the bulbous, mud-brick Emin Minaret, the ruins of abandoned towns and the 2000-year old Karez underground irrigation channels.

Kashgar

The fabled crossroads of central Asia, Kashgar lies 800 km (497 miles) from Urumqi, close to the borders of five other countries—Kyrgyzstan, Tajikistan, Afghanistan, Pakistan and India—and frequently fought over in the past.

The old town is a maze of twisting alleys leading off the central square, dominated by the great 15th-century Id Kah Mosque. The bazaars are full of local crafts: carpets, decorated chests, brass and copperware, jewellery and colourful clothing. Sunday is the big day in Kashgar, when tens of thousands of tribal people pour in from near and far. Processions of donkey carts, flocks of sheep and goats, camels and horses jam the market area to the east of the centre.

The Silk Road divided at Kashgar, one branch going west through central Asia, another south to Tashkurgan and over the 4720 m (15,500 ft) Khunjerab Pass. Today that is the route of the spectacular Karakoram Highway between Kashgar and Islamabad in Pakistan.

A close shave in the open air at Kashgar's famous market.

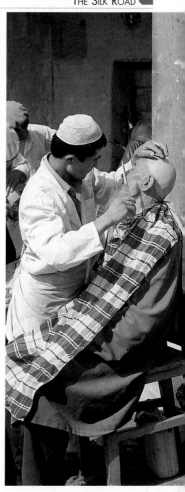

NANJING AND THE YANGTZE

Yangtze Bridge, Nanjing Sights, Zijinshan, Huangshan, Yangtze River Cruises, Chengdu

As capital and biggest city of Jiangsu province, Nanjing is one of China's most important commercial and industrial centres. For long periods in the past it was the capital of the whole of China, known in the west as Nanking (its name means "southern capital"), and the scene of some apocalyptic events. Nanjing was the first big city to fall to the extraordinary Taiping rebels, in 1853, amid horrific scenes of bloodshed. It was the centre of their Heavenly Kingdom until 1864, when the imperial army (with foreign help) finally crushed the rebellion, with huge loss of life and innumerable executions. Even these enormities were exceeded in 1937, when the invading Japanese forces captured the city and massacred vast numbers of its inhabitants in an atrocity known as the Rape of Nanking. The bodies were never counted, but estimates range up to 300,000, the figure given by Chinese authorities.

The city had been capital from the 3rd to the 6th centuries and again under the early Ming emperors, from 1368 to 1420. When Sun Yatsen founded the Republic of China in 1911 it resumed the role. After World War II, it was the seat of Chiang Kaishek's Nationalist government until the victorious Communists restored Beijing as capital in 1949.

Yangtze Bridge

The Yangtze (the Chiangjiang or "Long River") flows from the southwest, curving round Nanjing and heading east to the sea. Near the city, where it narrows to about 900 m (1000 yd), it is spanned by the two-tier Yangtze River Bridge—the pride of the People's Republic when it was completed in 1968, after Russian help had been withdrawn. The road bridge on the upper deck, with its approaches, is 4.6 km (3 miles) long; the rail bridge below stretches for 6.8 km (over 4 miles). This is the most important north-south link in China, and often congested. Another bridge is under construction.

Nanjing Sights

Within the arc of the Yangtze and its tributary the Qinhuai, dotted with lakes, parks, gardens and open spaces and surrounded by wooded hills, Nanjing today is one of the more agreeable of China's big cities. It has no single focus, but several separate centres scattered over a huge area.

47

City Walls

The first city walls were built in about 500 BC and frequently strengthened; traces of them can be seen at Stone City, near the west train station. Also visible are the crumbling ruins of the Stone Citadel dating from the Wu kingdom in the 3rd century AD, so worn and overgrown that they look like a natural hill.

The first Ming emperor, Hongwu, ordered the construction of a new and stronger wall. Built of brick by 200,000 labourers, it was 33 km (21 miles) long, making Nanjing the biggest walled city in the world. Large sections of it are still standing, as well as three massive gates. The largest is the southern gate, Zhonghuamen, four consecutive arches defended by a fortress which once housed a garrison of 3000.

Yuhuatai Park

Outside the south gate in Yuhuatai Park, Rain Flower Terrace takes its name from the pebbles of semi-precious stone, mainly agate, found on this low hill. The colours and patterns show up best when wetted—hence the name.

Taiping Museum

To the north of Zhonghuamen in Zhanyuan imperial garden, the Museum of the Taiping Heavenly Kingdom records the history of that strange interlude from 1853–64 when the visionary (or madman) Hong Xiuquan ruled as much as half of China from Nanjing.

To the north, near the crossing of Taiping Avenue and Zhongshan East Avenue, two of the city's main north-south and east-west streets, is his palace, later the Presidential Mansion of Sun Yatsen. It's an odd hybrid of western neoclassical and Chinese styles, painted in yellow and white.

Drum Tower

The restored Ming era Drum Tower which used to sound the hours and warn of danger is a landmark at another major intersection, that of Beijing Road and Zhongyang Road.

Nanjing Museum

Inside the East Gate (*Zhongshanmen*), the Nanjing Museum is one of China's best, despite the fact that the Nationalists took many of its treasures with them to Taiwan. From prehistoric artefacts, including a fabulous jade burial suit, its exhibits cover the art, ceramics, textiles and other crafts of all the whole imperial era as well as subsequent history.

Zijinshan

Most of Nanjing's sights are scattered over the Purple Hills, east of the centre.

Sun Yatsen Mausoleum

Sun Yatsen's tomb (*Zhongshanling*) was completed in 1929, four years after the leader's death. It stands on a wooded hillside; almost 400 white marble steps lead up to an imposing granite building with a blue-tiled roof.

Linggusi

To the east of the mausoleum, this is an active temple with monks in residence. It was an important Buddhist monastery in the Ming period; the Beamless Hall (1381), with a roof formed of a single unsupported brick arch 38 m (125 ft) high and 78 m (256 ft) long, is the only large building to survive from that era.

A path through the trees to the north leads to the National Cemetery where the names are listed of over 33,000 soldiers killed in the Northern Expedition of 1926–7 when Nationalist forces crushed rebellious warlords. The nine-storey pagoda in traditional style was built in 1929.

Tomb of the First Ming Emperor

To the west of the Sun Yatsen Mausoleum, closer to the city, is the Tomb of Hongwu, the first Ming emperor (also called Zhu Yuanzhang). The word tomb understates the concept; this was a vast compound, with pavilions, temples, halls, bridges and gardens, all enclosed within a wall, 22 km (14 miles) long. The wall and many of the buildings were destroyed during the Taiping period. Winding towards the tomb is the Sacred Way, a wooded path lined by pairs of giant statues of animals—elephants, lions and two-humped camels. The remains of the tomb itself are still imposing, with great brick arches, carved memorial stones weighing many tonnes and walls with traces of the vermilion paint which once covered them.

Huangshan

Immortalized by generations of poets and painters, Huangshan (Yellow Mountain) is a cluster of peaks, officially 72, in Anhui province, 240 km (150 miles) south of Nanjing. Not only scenic but sacred, they attract hosts of tourists and pilgrims. Flights of stone steps go close to the top of Lotus Flower peak, more than 1,850 m (6,070 ft) high, or you can take a cable car to one of the highest points. It's worth getting up early to see the sun rise on a magical panorama of dozens of pinnacles standing out like islands from a sea of cloud. Energetic hikers can follow well-marked tracks to several of the summits. As a bonus, there are hot springs waiting to soothe their tired muscles at the end of the day.

Yangtze River Cruises

A voyage along China's historic artery, the mighty Yangtze (or Yangzi), is a uniquely rewarding experience. The scenic section through the Three Gorges between Wuhan and Chongqing is the most popular, taking about five days going upstream, or three days downstream with the fast-flowing current, for the 1350 km (842 miles) journey.

Visitor traffic is on the increase; there's a rush to see the gorges before a huge dam, already under construction, inundates much of the area beneath a reservoir 600 km (375 miles) long. Cruise boats will be able to pass through at any stage up to the projected completion date of 2009, and after that, ocean-going vessels up to 10,000 tonnes will be able to reach Chongqing.

Wuhan to Wushan

Spreading over both banks, **Wuhan** is capital of Hubei Province. Wuchang, one of the city's three main districts, was a former capital of the state of Wu during the Three Kingdoms period (the other kingdoms were Shu and Wei). Hankou, the northern district, became a treaty port in the 19th century, and picturesque concession architecture survives near the waterfront.

On the west bank, the **Guiyuan Temple** in Hanyang has an impressive altar in the main hall, the reverse of which is occupied by a glittering statue of Guanyin, the Buddhist Goddess of Mercy. Another hall hosts a congregation of 500 Luohan statues. The Luohan (usually seen in two ranks of nine) are those who have been freed from the Buddhist cycle of

rebirth. The large pool in the first courtyard of the temple testifies to the Chinese feng shui belief that bad spirits are unable to cross water. Note the carved lotus flowers in the pool, Buddhist symbols of transcendence.

On the east bank, **Chairman Mao's Villa**, near the East Lake in Wuchang, is a rather doleful memento of the Great Helmsman's frequent stays in the city, but essential viewing for devotees of recent Chinese history. The nearby **Hubei Provincial Museum** has an excellent collection of artefacts culled from the grave of the Marquis of Zeng, who was buried in 433 BC. The display includes a magnificent set of bells—one of the most appealing museum collections in the land. Also in Wuchang on Snake Hill by the river, the heavily restored

Yellow Crane Pavilion was eulogized in a famous Tang dynasty poem.

The wide river upstream from Wuhan teems with barges and ferries heading east. Cruises often disembark their passengers at the port city of **Yueyang** (nine hours from Wuhan) to view the Yueyang Tower, first built during the Three Kingdom period. This is Hunan (South of the Lakes) Province, home to some of China's spiciest food, so it's worth seeking out a roadside restaurant for a taste test. Yueyang sits alongside China's second largest freshwater lake, Dongting.

The flat land upstream from Yueyang leads you back into Hubei (North of the Lakes) Province and to the industrial town of Shashi. The nearby city of **Jingzhou** is girdled by a wall

last rebuilt during the Qing dynasty.

Further upstream, **Yichang** is a major port for freight moving along the Yangtze. The city dates back from the Sui dynasty and served for a period as a foreign treaty port. There is not much to see today in Yichang, but a number of tours of the Three Gorges begin or end here.

The city's most famous attraction is the nearby **Gezhou Dam** 4 km (2.5 miles) upstream which was completed in 1988. The Chinese tend to get very excited about massive civil engineering feats, and the Gezhou Dam— 2,561 m (8,400 ft) long, 70 m (230 ft) high and 30 m (98 ft) wide—is no exception. A railway and road run across it. Two sluice gates shunt silt downstream to prevent it from building up behind the dam; without them, the river upstream would completely silt up after around 100 years. The dam is currently Chi-

THREE GORGES DAM

Originally dreamed up by Republican father Sun Yatsen, later championed by Mao Zedong and then railroaded through the National People's Congress in 1992 by Li Peng, the Three Gorges Dam, if completed, will be the largest hydroelectric dam in the world. Apart from churning out kilowatts, the dam will also play an important role in flood prevention, and navigability upstream will be dramatically improved. Straddling the Yangtze, the dam will create a reservoir more than 563 km (350 miles) long, whose waters will lap at the shores of Chongqing, forcing the relocation of up to 2 million people. The Three Gorges will be submerged, leaving only their peaks as islets above water; submarine tours could take over from surface vessels.

Work began on the US $20 billion project in 1994, and is expected to be completed by 2009. Accusations have flown that land has been illegally grabbed, creating vast numbers of refugees, that official relocation is well behind target, and that corruption has seriously compromised safety standards (at least one official in charge of the dam has been sentenced to death). The disappearance of the Three Gorges will be an inestimable loss. However, the Communist Party's prestige depends totally on the dam's success; any drastic mishap would be seen as an equivalent—and almost certainly irreparable—failure of government credibility.

na's largest hydroelectric power generator and plays an important role in flood protection.

Another 40 km (25 miles) upstream from Yichang, you will find the construction of the gargantuan **Three Gorges Dam** *(Sanxiaba)* in full throttle. The colossal engineering endeavour has churned the land around Sandouping into a lunarscape of construction debris. The hydroelectric output of the Three Gorges Dam will eclipse that of the Gezhou Dam. For the curious, buses can be taken from Yichang to visit the construction site.

The scenic **Three Gorges** *(Sanxia)* begin once your boat drifts past Nanjin Pass, a bend in the river of great strategic importance during the Three Kingdoms period and after.

Xiling Gorge is the longest of the three at 76 km (47 miles). It was famously a treacherous obstacle course and greatly feared, with vessels smashing onto hidden rocks, going down on hazardous shoals, snarling reefs, swift rapids or whirling eddies. The shoals were created by landslides from the crumbling precipices above, but now the most dangerous rocks have been removed through blasting. However, landslides still occur occasionally.

Xiling Gorge bristles with legend. Huangling Temple, nestling at the foot of Nine Dragon Hill by Yellow Ox Rock, is the oldest building in the gorges. Its history is said to date back to the Spring and Autumn Period (771–476 BC), when it was called the Ox Temple. It was later renovated by Zhuge Liang, a master strategist of the Three Kingdom period.

PACIFYING THE DEMONS

There is a Chinese saying, "Xiling's shoals are dense as bamboo joints, even ghosts look anxiously at each one". Qingtan (Green Shoals) and Kongling were the most worrisome rapids, but dredging and dynamite has tamed them. The most famous submerged stone in Kongling, named "Here it Comes!" wilfully lured boats into its path; other notorious hazards were the Pearl, the Second Pearl and Third Pearl. Safe passage depended on the water level, high in summer and low in winter, when the rocks were exposed. In ages past, boatsmen would stand on the bows and wave a flag inscribed with Chinese characters to pacify the demons of the water; another technique was to sprinkle grains of rice on the river throughout the rapids.

Many sights along the way are named after formations, clefts and splits in the rock that appear to imitate animals, mythical creatures or objects. Some of them are easy to recognize, but it will take a vivid imagination to discern Ox's Liver and Horse's Lung Gorge.

In Shadowplay Gorge, a stretch of caves and waterfalls, four rocks relate to characters from the *Journey to the West*, a famous epic that relates how the Buddhist scriptures came to China from India. One of the rocks is thought to resemble the great Tang dynasty explorer Xuanzang, who made his way to India via China's mighty northwest, returning with bundles of Buddhist *sutras*.

The Sword and Military Strategy Book Gorge, a heap of rocks that looks like a pile of books with a sword next to it, is associated with Zhuge Liang.

The Fragrant Stream empties into the great Yangtze, marking the end of Xiling Gorge. Ahead lies the town of **Zigui**, a place of great significance to the Chinese for it was the birthplace of one of the country's greatest poets and statesmen—Qu Yuan (c. 343–280 BC). His verse characteristically jostles with spirits, demons and witches, and his death is marked annually by Dragon Boat races.

Beyond Zigui is the entrance to the **Wu Gorge** (Gorge of the Witches) at Guandukou. The river here is dramatically bordered by towering peaks and steep cliff walls that eclipse the sun and bathe the gorge in shadow. The gorge, 40 km (25 miles) long, takes its name from Wushan (Mount Wu), and its twelve peaks that dominate this section. Wushan is a stirring mountain, especially when shrouded in cloud and mist. The play of sunlight on the haze that drifts between the looming peaks creates a mysterious and almost paranormal landscape. Here and there the rock is split and needled into fantastic shafts. Most travellers consider this the most sombre of the Three Gorges.

The twelve peaks of Wushan lie on either side of the Yangtze. To the north are Denglong (Climbing Dragon), Shengquan (Holy Spring), Chaoyun (Facing Clouds), Shennu (Fairy), Songluan (Pine Mountain) and Jixian (Gathering of Immortals); and to the south stand Juhe (Flock of Cranes), Cuiping (Emerald Green Screen) and Feifeng (Flying Phoenix). Three other peaks lie beyond sight. A legend associated with Wushan tells that the twelve peaks are animated by the souls of fairies. The spirit of Yaoji, daughter of the Queen of Heaven, was captured in the peak of Shennu, after she descended to earth to help the mythical Great Yu in his creation of the Three Gorges.

The curtain falls on Wu Gorge with Golden Helmet and Silver Armour Gorge, where the fractured and layered cliff walls are said to resemble ancient Chinese battledress.

Cruise ships often dock overnight in **Wushan**, hometown of the mythical Great Yu who is said to have harnessed the perennial floods and created the Three Gorges thousands of years ago. You are now in Sichuan (Four Rivers) Province, homeland of the world famous Sichuan cuisine (*chuancai* in Chinese). Fiercely hot and spicy, it differs from Hunan food in its liberal use of a distinctive, numbing herb.

Daning River

You may want to take a trip on a sampan down the Daning (Great Peace) River from Wushan and through the **Little Three Gorges**; this should be possible as long as the water is not too high. The Daning River originates in Shaanxi Province to the north. A saying puts it thus: "Returning from the five (Taoist) peaks, there is no need to see other mountains; returning from Daning River, there's no need to see other gorges"; in other words, they are unsurpassed. Indeed, the stream is narrow, and the Little Three Gorges can be considered more picturesque and impressive than their larger siblings on the Yangtze. The vegetation on the mountains on either side is lush and, especially in the right light, the water fresh and sparkling. The complete length of the Three Little Gorges is around 60 km (37 miles).

The first is **Longmen** (Dragon Gate) **Gorge**, which, at 3 km (under 2 miles) is the shortest of the three. It begins with towering precipices that open like a huge door. Bamboo rustles on the banks and the Longmen Spring gurgles into the river. Leaving the gorge, you will ride past the furious Yinwo Shoals, where the river rages and foams.

Tieguan (Iron Coffin) **Gorge** is 10 km (6 miles) long, and replete with strange rock formations that have been given fanciful animal names. On a ledge on the eastern precipice is a black coffin which belongs to a tribe called the Ba. It has been here since the time of the Warring States (476–221 BC). You will see more coffins later in the last of the large Three Gorges.

Dicui Gorge (Dripping Emerald Gorge) is the most attractive and longest of the three, at 20 km (12 miles) long. It has lush greenery and monkeys gibbering from the forest branches. 55

Sections of the Daning River are exhilarating, energetic torrents, and on occasion you may have to disembark to make your way along the riverbank while your boat battles against the flow. Return trips along the Daning from Wushan take 5–6 hours.

Wushan to Chongqing

Back on the Yangtze, the last of the Three Gorges, **Qutang**, lies ahead. The gorge is the shortest at 8 km (5 miles), but is considered the most spectacular and thrilling. At its narrowest point, it constricts the flow of the Yangtze to a mere 50 m (164 ft), the water consequently deepening and flowing more rapidly between the cliffs towering on either side.

At **Fengxiang** (Bellows) **Gorge**, near the eastern access to Qutang and high on the northern cliff face, is a series of crevices where a collection of coffins was found. These are also attributed to the Ba who used the ledges for burial. For centuries, voyagers imagined that the coffins were boxes that contained the bellows of a carpenter, Lu Ban, who assisted the Great Yu in his dredging of the river. It was not until 1971 that the cliff was scaled and the

The Daning River at Dragon Gate Bridge: the waters have now been raised by 60 m.

"boxes" opened, revealing their human remains, swords, combs and other artefacts.

Not far downstream and on the opposite side of the river, you will see the **Mengliang Ladder**, a series of holes made in the rock. These originally contained piles that were driven into the rock face, which in turn supported a pathway. You can also see another type of pathway cut out of the rock. Gangs would drag heavy junks loaded with goods upstream by ropes against the current, overseen by "gangers" armed with sticks who would regularly beat slackers.

The Monk Hanging Upside Down is a realistic geological oddity resembling a suspended figure, and the rock known as the Rhinoceros Gazing at the Moon is similarly lifelike.

The Whitewashed Walls on the cliff face of Mount Baiyan at **Kuimen** are carved with Chinese calligraphy. These inscriptions date from the Song dynasty, vary in size from the minute to the massive, and extend from short pronouncements to complete texts from the Chinese classics.

Further upstream, at the western entrance to Qutang Gorge, five huge Chinese characters sail into view. They translate as "Kuimen is the mightiest (pass) in the entire world". Near the entrance to Qutang Gorge once stood a notorious rock that claimed the lives of many boatmen, but it was blasted in the 20th century.

Just beyond Kuimen is **Baidicheng** (White King Town). China's two most famous poets of the Tang dynasty, Li Bai and Du Fu, lived just upstream at Fengjie. Both poets frequently praised the great river in song, the most famous being Li Bai's recollection of his departure downriver:

In the morning, I leave Baidi between colourful clouds,
A thousand miles of river and land, to return the next day.
On each bank the gibbons scream without pause
My boat has already drifted past endless hills.

Baidicheng, on White King Mountain, dates from the Western Han dynasty (206 BC–AD 23) and was originally called Purple Sun Town. It was renamed when the ruler of the area now known as Sichuan Province, Gong Sunshu, saw vapour emerging from a well like a white dragon soaring up into the sky. The town is most famous among Chinese for a pivotal moment in the history of the Three Kingdoms. Liu Bei, ruler of the kingdom of Shu (the old name for Sichuan) attacked the kingdom of Wu to avenge the murder of his brother, Guan Yu, against the advice of master strategist Zhuge Liang. The attack failed catastrophically and Liu retreated to Baidicheng. On his deathbed, Liu entrusted Zhuge Liang with control of his kingdom, a scene that is represented by statues in the White King Temple.

The ancient walled town of **Fengjie** is popularly called the Poetry Town because of its association with Li Bai and Du Fu. It formerly had a reputation for its manufacture of salt. To the east is Zhuge Liang's Eight Battle Array Formation at the mouth of the Meixi River. This collection of stones and rocks trapped large numbers of Wu troops. Around Fengjie you will see numerous

---

RIVER BURIALS

While on your journey along the Yangtze River, you could well see the occasional body floating downstream, strapped to a bamboo raft. Despite being undeniably grisly, there is nothing more sinister to this than an inexpensive alternative to burial on land. This is still a common and eerie sight, with the body being ferried through rapids to its unknown destination. Such sightings are a poignant reminder that the great river has historically delivered both life and death to those who live along its shores.

other geological oddities, caves and caverns (including the Black Wind Cave).

Fengjie and Baidicheng together mark the end of the Three Gorges, but there is still a long stretch of river between here and Chongqing. **Wanxian** is an attractive staging post for boats ploughing the route. It is at the centre of a citrus-growing area and famous for cane and rattan furniture and basketry.

Shibaozhai (Stone Treasure Storehouse) upstream is a towering rock resembling a Chinese seal-chop, capped with a red 11-storey pagoda-shaped temple.

Fengdu, the City of Ghosts, is a spectral stop further upriver. Vessels used to moor in midstream to fend off the spooks. Ming Mountain sports temples to Yinwang, China's God of the Underworld.

The end of your voyage is the huge city of **Chongqing**, now a municipality like Beijing, Tianjin and Shanghai. The Yangtze and Jialing rivers meet here in a vast confluence; boats usually moor at the Chaotianmen Docks at the division of the two streams.

Chongqing was opened as a treaty port in the late 19th century. Nationalist (Kuomingtang/ KMT) capital during the war with Japan (1937–45), it was badly bombed by the Japanese airforce and much of its history destroyed.

The city is almost unique in China in that there are virtually no bicycles due to its steep streets.

In his book *The River of Golden Sand* (1883), Captain William Gill narrates how, while in Chongqing, Chinese threw stones at his photographer's camera. They believed that foreigners used a juice made from children's eyes to produce photographs! Today, Chongqing seethes with industry and steams under the sun. It is known as one of the "Three Furnaces" of China, along with Wuhan and Nanjing. The inhabitants intensify the heat by slurping what is surely the city's greatest success story: the hotpot (*huoguo*). This searing concoction is China's spiciest formula, and highly recommended. There is no better place to sample it. The soup (*tang*) arrives in a hotpot, often divided into two sections: hot (*la*) and not hot (*bu la*). You fling into the boiling cauldron everything that the waitress places on your table: *doufu*, crabs, mushrooms, lamb strips, cabbage and more.

Apart from a scattering of political monuments and sights associated with Communist and KMT history, Chongqing stands shorn of much of its past. The venerable Buddhist Luohan Temple on Minzu Lu guards a population of 500 lifelike statues similar to those in Wuhan.

59

Chengdu

Landlocked Sichuan is China's most productive interior province. Chengdu, the capital is lively and pleasant and not as daunting as a population of 4 million (9 million including suburbs and satellites) might suggest. Apart from its own attractions and famously tasty food, it's a good base for visits to some historic highlights in the region.

The city centre is marked by an enormous statue of Chairman Mao, gazing benignly south along the main avenue, Renmin Nanlu. There are plenty of animated markets, including one for antiques and crafts in Cultural Park, west of the centre.

Tours of Chengdu usually include a visit to the Dufu Thatched Cottage, a museum and shrine to the Tang dynasty poet Dufu who lived at this spot in the 8th century. The present thatched pavilion probably bears little relation to his turf-roofed hut.

Wenshusi, with its working monastery, is the city's most active temple, highly decorated, packed with worshippers and dense with smoke.

Panda Research Centre

Chengdu has had some success breeding pandas in captivity: the centre north of the city is not open to the general public but some groups are allowed access.

Dujiangyan

At Guanxian, 60 km (37 miles) northwest of Chengdu, Dujiangyan is a famous flood control and irrigation scheme originally built in the 3rd century BC. Amazingly, it is still in working order, irrigating over 3 million ha. It was designed by a local governor, Li Bing; a temple in the lovely park at the site has a statue of him erected as a tribute in AD 168.

Leshan

A 3-hour drive from Chengdu takes you to Leshan, 180 km to the southwest. Here amid lush mountain scenery, three rivers converge and flow past the walls of the old market town. Carved into the sandstone cliffs of the opposite bank is the colossal Dafo or Giant Buddha, a seated figure 71 m (233 ft) tall. Begun in AD 713, it took the monks over 90 years to complete. Boats ferry visitors across the river to land near its feet; hundreds of steps lead up to viewing points at the top of the cliff.

Emeishan

At over 3,000 m (9,900 ft) high, Emeishan, 40 km (25 miles) west of Leshan, is one of China's four holiest mountains, and one of its most beautiful. Unless you are equipped for the long hike to the top, you'll have to be content to view it from below.

A sea of clouds drifts around the summit of Emeishan.

◆ KUNMING

City Sights, Dian Lake, Western Hills,
Shilin Stone Forest, Yunnan Excursions

Kunming is the capital and biggest city of Yunnan, China's southwestern province, bordering Vietnam, Laos and Myanmar (Burma). An altitude of 1900 m (6230 ft) gives it a pleasant summer average temperature of 20°C (68°F). With mild winters, too, it has been labelled the City of Eternal Spring.

Yunnan became part of China as late as the 13th century, when the Mongol rulers of the empire added it to their conquests. It remained isolated from the rest of the country by difficult mountain terrain, often in the hands of bandits. An easier route lay to the southeast, along the Red River to Indo-China (Vietnam), especially after the completion of the French-built railway from Kunming to Haiphong in 1910. Two years earlier, Kunming had been opened to foreign trade, effectively under French control.

When Japan invaded China in 1937 and seized the coastal provinces, many wealthy Chinese fled to Kunming. Whole industrial plants and educational institutes relocated there, and the city expanded rapidly. When the Japanese also occupied Vietnam and Burma, aid for the Chinese Nationalists was flown in "over the hump" by heavily laden US and British planes labouring across the Himalayas from India. Expansion continued under the People's Republic, but Kunming fared badly during the Cultural Revolution; as a former Nationalist stronghold, its leaders were suspected of deviation. Paradoxically, many victims who were banished to Kunming from other cities liked it so much they decided to stay. Today, over a million people live in the city, and three times that number in the whole urban area. Major products include copper, steel, trucks, chemicals and optical equipment; telescopes are a speciality.

City Sights

Wide tree-shaded avenues slice across the centre, with a maze of narrow alleys leading off them. Kunming's flower and bird markets are famed for variety, and there's a wide choice of restaurants—try the Yunnan speciality "across-the-bridge" noodles (a spicy hotpot) and the goats' cheese, a rarity in China.

The Yunnan Provincial Museum houses impressive 2400-year old bronzes from tombs near Kunming, together with displays illustrating the costumes and traditions of the province's minority peoples. Northeast of the centre, set in floral gardens, the Golden Temple (*Jindian*) from the early Qing period (17th century) shows Daoist, Buddhist and Confucian influences.

Dian Lake

South of the city, Dian Lake (*Dianchi*) stretches for 50 km (30 miles). At the Village of Ethnic Culture on the northeastern shore, representatives of 26 different tribes from all parts of Yunnan demonstrate crafts and stage song and dance shows.

East of the lake is a land of fruit orchards and flower nurseries growing azaleas, camellias and hundreds of varieties of orchids.

Western Hills

Northwest of the lake, the land rises steeply, with a succession of temples punctuating the path to the top. The most important, the Buddhist Huating Temple, was originally a retreat for Kunming's rulers, before the Mongol conquest. Hundreds of vivid ceramic statues line the main hall.

High above the lake, Dragon Gate (*Longmen*) is reached by meandering steps cut and tunnelled into a high cliff. Grottoes in the mountainside contain painted statues carved in the 18th century by Daoist monks.

Shilin Stone Forest

Thousands of tall pillars of limestone rock, eroded into fantastic shapes and interspersed with trees, cover an area of 300 sq km (over 100 sq miles), 120 km (75 miles) to the southeast of Kunming. As usual in China, many of the pillars are given fanciful names. There's a superb view from the Peak Viewing Pavilion, but no solitude in which to savour it; this is a major tourist magnet. The Sani people who live in the area pose for photos, sell colourful embroidery, and stage music and dance shows at the tourist hotels.

Yunnan Excursions

Flights of less than an hour from Kunming can take you to mountain resorts, nature reserves with exotic flora and fauna, and the homelands of some of Yunnan's varied ethnic groups.

Lijiang

Northwest of Kunming in the foothills of the Himalayas, Lijiang stands in a lovely valley with Jade Dragon Snow Mountain as a dramatic backdrop. A maze of narrow streets and ramshackle wooden buildings, the old town is the home of the Naxi people, a matriarchal society where women own the property and run businesses while men provide the entertainment. The 63 celebrated Lijiang Naxi orchestra has miraculously preserved the music of a thousand years ago, forgotten in the rest of China.

The ancient town of Baisha, 10 km (6 miles) to the north, was the Naxi capital before the Mongol conquest and is still a centre of Naxi culture.

Dali

With a spectacular wall of mountain peaks to the west and Erhai Lake, 40 km (25 miles) long to the east, Dali's perfect location has made it a favourite escape from Kunming. The picturesque old walled town has 9th-century pagodas, lively markets and the region's colourful Bai people.

Xishuangbanna

Southwest of Kunming, close to the border with Myanmar, is a vast and verdant wonderland of lush rainforest, gorgeous flowers, tea plantations and green paddy fields. Flights land at the main town, Jinghong, which draws many visitors to its April Dai Water-Splashing Festival.

Canals thread through Lijiang's old streets.

SHANGHAI AND THE GRAND CANAL

The Bund, Pudong, Nanjing Road, Old City,
Western Shanghai, Suzhou, Wuxi,
Lake Tai, Hangzhou, Ningbo

At the peak of the building boom in the 1990s, it was said that a quarter of the construction cranes in the *world* were at work in Shanghai. With an official population of over 13 million, this dynamic city is growing at astonishing speed. And the skyline changes just as quickly, especially in Pudong, across the Huangpu river from the historic Bund.

Shanghai grew up as a centre of river and coastal commerce; by the 16th century it had strong walls to protect it from pirates. It was one of the first five Treaty Ports opened to foreign trade in the 1840s. First the British, then the French and later half a dozen other nations acquired concessions (in effect small colonies) which eventually added up to the International Settlement, larger in area than the Chinese city.

In the free-wheeling 1920s, Shanghai was famous as a hotbed of vice and crime, where miscreants could flit from one district to another to evade the law. The end came suddenly, in 1937, when Japanese forces bombed and then occupied the city. In 1941 they rounded up and interned many foreign nationals. After World War II and the defeat of Japan, there was a brief interlude under Chiang Kaishek's Nationalists when traders tried to take up where they had left off. In 1949 everything changed again, when Communist troops marched in, the People's Republic was established and businesses were closed or nationalized. The new government was suspicious of Shanghai's former "cosmopolitanism" (a dirty word) and kept its people on a tight rein, but could not do without their know-how. Industry was expanded, causing appalling pollution problems, only reduced in recent years by relocating factories away from the centre. The Cultural Revolution hit hard here, but creativity and initiative were not dead, only dormant. When Deng Xiaoping liberalized economic policy in the 1980s, Shanghai was ready to respond. Contacts with overseas investors were resumed, new businesses mushroomed, hotels opened. Unthinkable only a few years before, General Motors built a factory to produce Buick cars!

The Bund

An old Anglo-Indian word for an embankment, the Bund is Shanghai's famous waterfront where an arc of impressive European buildings faces the wide, muddy-brown Huangpu river. Although they date from the period of imperialist domination, Shanghai is proud of these relics and determined to preserve them. One of the most imposing, the former headquarters of the Hongkong and Shanghai Bank, opened in 1923. It was turned into the City Hall after the Communist victory of 1949, but is now the Pudong Development Bank. Don't miss the chance to look inside—it's open every day—to see the palatial banking hall with its soaring marble columns and allegorical mosaics, all in pristine condition.

Peace Hotel

Originally the Cathay, the hotel on the corner of Nanjing Road is said to be where Noel Coward wrote part of *Private Lives*. In the early years of the People's Republic it hosted party bigwigs and high-level foreign delegations. Walk through the lobby to see a jewel of Art Deco design, well-restored, and take a drink on the 8th floor terrace for a fine view of the river and the city, old and new. At night, the lights along the Bund and across the river make a spectacular show.

Huangpu Park

Across the street from the Peace Hotel, Huangpu Park is a popular spot for strolling, being photographed, playing cards, having a haircut or a medical consultation. Early in the morning it's full of people practising *tai chi* or even line dancing. Boats from the nearby wharf will take you on a relaxed 3-hour cruise along the river past the varied shipping, docks, container terminals and constructions sites, down to where the Huangpu reaches the mouth of the mighty Yangtze, so wide it feels like the open sea.

Pudong

In sharp contrast to the Bund, the skyline of the Pudong New Area across the river rivals Hong Kong and Singapore. Rising 90 floors and more from flat former marshland are futuristic towers and pinnacles of tinted glass and glittering metal: luxury hotels including the world's tallest, offices and apartments. Topping them all—so far—is the Oriental Pearl TV tower, 468 m (1536 ft) high, like a needle impaling a set of spheres (the pearls). The view from the highest is another must for the hosts of visitors from all parts of China and beyond. Away in the mist to the east is Pudong's new international airport, built to handle 20 million passengers a year.

Nanjing Donglu is Shanghai's glitziest shopping street.

Nanjing Road

Running west from the Bund, Nanjinglu was the city's main commercial street in the days of the foreign concessions. Today it provides the evidence of China's conversion to consumerism. Its department stores, fashion boutiques, restaurants and garishly lit fast food outlets rival those of Tokyo or Hong Kong.

Shanghai Museum

On the south side of Nanjing Road, 2.5 km (1.5 miles) west of the Bund, is the People's Park and People's Square area. It was a racetrack until the 1930s, and later the site of huge political rallies. Now it's partly park, with shopping malls on lower levels and, in the southern half, Shanghai's new museum, shaped like a bronze urn on a tripod. Opened in 1996, it is one of the biggest and best in China, with fine collections of ceramics from every era, bronzes, calligraphy and furniture, displayed on five floors.

Grand Theatre

On the northwest corner of People's Park, the glass and steel Grand Theatre is topped by a great curving roof symbolizing the infinite sky. Built by French architect Jean-Marie Charpentier, who also designed the Opéra Bastille in Paris, it was completed in 1998.

Old City

In the days of the foreign concessions, the Chinese city lay just inland of the southern end of the Bund. Nowadays it blends into adjoining areas but shows up on city maps as a circle of roads following the line of an ancient, long-vanished wall. Several of Shanghai's biggest tourist magnets are clustered at its northern end.

Yuyuan Garden

A remarkable survival, this is a classical Chinese garden of pools, bridges, moon-gates, latticed pavilions and rockeries, dating from the 16th century.

Next to the garden is the two-storey Huxinting Tea House, where you can sip all sorts of tea and listen to Chinese music.

Old Market

Such traces of traditional China are rare in a city which is essentially a creation of the 19th and 20th centuries. Seeing a chance to capitalize on nostalgia, a tycoon based in Singapore has invested in the modern facsimile of an old market district, with tiny shops and stalls, right next to the entrance to the Yuyuan Garden. From diminutive street stalls to thousand-seat dim sum restaurants, the eating opportunities here and all over Shanghai are endless.

Western Shanghai

The tree-lined streets of the former French concession hint of an elegance which is returning as the area becomes the fashionable place to live. Among new luxury apartment buildings that would not look out of place in the more exclusive districts of Paris, you can still spot some of the original villas.

Historical Villas

In July 1921, Mao Zedong and a dozen fellow delegates gathered in one of these residences to found the Chinese Communist Party. French police got wind of the meeting but the conspirators made their escape and continued their discussions on a boat. The villa has been preserved as a national monument to the First National Congress and contains a small exhibition. It has recently been renovated, and an artificial lake is being constructed opposite, where a replica of the boat will be anchored. Around the villa, the old district of narrow lanes and stone houses has been entirely transformed into a shopping and leisure centre, Xintiandi (New Earth and Sky), incorporating offices, conference rooms, hotels and apartment blocks.

To the west of the Congress villa, across Fuxing Park, the former residence of Dr Sun Yatsen (Zhongshan) is another political shrine, preserving many relics of the founder of the Republic. Yet another historic figure, Mao's right-hand man Zhou Enlai lived just a block to the south of the park in a comfortable old-fashioned house with a small garden.

Jade Buddha Temple

The Jade Buddha temple on Anyuan Road, hemmed in by tall buildings northwest of the city centre, was built as a monastery in 1882 to enshrine two statues of Buddha brought from Burma (Myanmar). One is life-size, seated, the other reclining, and each is carved from a single piece of precious white jade. It was closed during the Cultural Revolution, and protected from serious harm by displaying a portrait of Mao Zedong at the gate, which was guarded by soldiers posted there on the orders of Zhou Enlai. Now the temple is functioning again, with many resident monks and dense crowds of worshippers as well as processions of tourists.

Suzhou

Criss-crossed by canals and surrounded by a moat, the ancient city of Suzhou lies 84 km (52 miles) west of Shanghai in the flat and fertile province of Jiangsu. Marco Polo told of its splendours in the 13th century, labelling it the Venice of the East. He reported that its citizens were all dressed in silk, so prosperous had they become from the silk industry. From the 15th to the 19th centuries it was a centre of scholarship and the arts.

The old centre of Suzhou today is charming, with quiet canal-side walks, picturesque bridges, local markets and little houses. Sadly, many of these are threatened with destruction and replacement by new low-rise apartments, which the present occupants probably won't be able to afford.

Old City and Gardens

Suzhou is known as a city of gardens. They were created by Mandarin scholars and artists, mainly in the Ming and early Qing periods although some date from even earlier. Neglected, or used to house several families, in the 1920s and 30s, they were restored again in recent times, but some suffered damage in the Cultural Revolution. It is said that there were 400 during the Qing period, and 100 still survive.

Chinese gardens follow their own conventions: clumps of bamboo represent forests, rockeries serve as mountains, miniature waterfalls splash into ponds filled with colourful carp. Rocks from nearby Lake Tai, treated as individual treasures in Beijing's gardens, are here piled in profusion.

The Humble Administrator's Garden in the northern part of the old city is the largest in Suzhou, covering 4 hectares (10 acres) of ponds and pavilions, rock features and walks. In the southeast corner, the smaller but much older Garden of the Master of the Nets takes its name from its 12th century founder, a retired politician who said he preferred the life of a fisherman. It was restored in the 18th century, and in the 1920s became the home of two artists who famously kept a pet tiger there.

Panmen

At the southwest corner of the old city, Panmen (Pan Gate) is the last vestige of the old wall. Stone ramps lead to the top where it's possible to walk a short way. The architecture is echoed in the entrance to the nearby Sheraton Hotel. For the best view of the area and the canal traffic climb the stepped arch of Wumen Bridge just south of the gate.

Standing out in the flat landscape northwest of the moated city is Tiger Hill, an artificial mound created 2500 years ago. It is topped by a seven-storey pagoda, 1000 years old and leaning slightly from the vertical; it has been reinforced to prevent it from falling over.

Workshops

Outside the moat—the city wall has gone—Suzhou is more typical of China's big cities, with huge areas of identical tower blocks and industrial development old and new. Visitors are usually taken to see a silk factory filled with clattering machines and an embroidery workshop where young women create double-sided pictures formed from tiny stitches.

Singapore set up a special industrial zone (almost on the lines of the old international concessions) in the 1990s and attracted foreign companies to set up factories, notably pharmaceuticals and electronics. But the Suzhou authorities then set up another zone to undercut the Singaporeans, who withdrew most of their investment.

Hanshan Temple

A section of the Grand Canal passes to the west of Suzhou. Beside it stands Hanshan (Cold Mountain) Temple, made famous by the Tang Dynasty poet Zhang Ji. His lines:

Beyond the town of Suzhou stands Hanshansi;
the chime of its midnight bell reaches me as I lie in my boat

are memorized by Chinese and Japanese children at school, and many come to visit it in later life. Vast crowds flock here on New Year's Eve (both Western and Chinese versions). The elegant arch of Feng Bridge (*Fengqiao*) is another celebrated landmark.

Wuxi

When the tin mines which had led to its growth in the Bronze Age ran out of ore 2000 years ago, the town was given its present name, which just means 'no tin'. In the 7th century the Grand Canal brought trade and prosperity, but Wuxi has usually been overshadowed by its more famous neighbour Suzhou. It has a spacious modern centre near the railway station, just north of the old city which is still ringed by a moat, connected to the Grand Canal which skirts it to the west.

THE GRAND CANAL

As early as the 5th century BC, local rulers began to link lakes and rivers by way of canals. During the Sui dynasty (AD 581–618) the Yangtze and Yellow (Huanghe) rivers were joined, a distance of 400 km (250 miles). When the Mongol Yuan emperors moved the capital to Beijing in the 13th century, a route was needed to move grain from south to north. They ordered the digging of a canal from the Yellow River through northern Shandong to the Wei, near Tianjin, and another on to Beijing. Under the Ming dynasty it was widened and deepened; with extensions it amounted to almost 1800 km (1100 miles). The whole system remained in use until the 19th century, when rebellions disrupted canal traffic and prevented regular dredging, essential to clear the vast quantities of silt brought down by the rivers. Railways and coastal shipping took over the canal's role. Under the People's Republic the southern sections of the canal have been restored and new locks built; it is hoped eventually to reopen the entire length.

The 4-hour cruise from Suzhou to Wuxi is so packed with sights to see that many people stay on deck the whole way, ignoring the comfortable seats in the cabin.

Wonderfully ramshackle barges pass in a continuous procession, some so heavily laden with bricks, rocks, matting, cement, or waste cardboard that the water laps over their narrow decks. All of life goes on aboard, amid a clutter of pot plants, dogs, bicycles, cooking stoves and clothes hanging out to dry.

Three or even four rough-and-ready engines, each cooled by a tankful of canal water, topped up as required, drive belts and propellors at the stern. At any time you may see the bargeman doing running repairs on one, while the others keep the vessel moving. Some loads are so high and wide the man at the wheel can't see the way ahead through the heavy traffic, so his wife stands near the bow calling out directions.

One tug can pull up to fifteen loaded barges; how long would it take to stop such a train? Others tow rafts of timber—a dozen tree trunks lashed together—that have been travelling for so long that they've sprouted a garden of reeds and grass.

Close to the station, a bird, flower and antique market fills the lanes behind an active Buddhist temple, marked by a high pagoda roof.

Lake Tai

Visitors arrive on canal cruises from Suzhou, or come to see Lake Tai (*Taihu*), celebrated in poetry and legend and the source of many of the odd-shaped rocks that so fascinated garden designers. One of the biggest freshwater lakes in China, 68 km (42 miles) long, its clean fresh water is used for fish-farming and growing water chestnuts and the shores are planted with fruit orchards. You can take a boat trip among its dozens of islands, or climb the wooded hills around the lake, topped by temples, for romantically misty views. The lakeside is becoming fashionable among weekenders from Shanghai, who can play golf on a course designed by Jack Nicklaus.

Hangzhou

Poets and artists have been sighing over Hangzhou for more than a thousand years. Its West Lake (*Xihu*) is hailed as the most beautiful in China; Marco Polo reported that "a voyage on this lake offers more refreshment and delectation than any other experience on earth." If you think he exaggerated, take a sightseeing boat to one of its islands, or climb one of the hills on the western shore for a view of the whole lake—it's only about 3 km (2 miles) across.

The southern terminus of the Grand Canal (this section was completed in the 7th century), Hangzhou served as imperial capital from 1126 to 1279, during the Song Dynasty. Marco Polo was as enthusiastic about the city as its lake: "the finest and most splendid city in the world".

Silk and tea are the city's two most famous products, and today a museum is devoted to each of them. Longjing, southwest of the lake, is known for its green tea, grown on terraces surrounding the village.

Temple of Inspired Seclusion

Chinese tourists flock to Feilaifeng, a hill that stands about 3 km (2 miles) west of the lake. Here, the rock has been carved into hundreds of figures of Buddha, large and small, many of them laughing infectiously amid the foliage, or in natural or artificial caves.

Lingyinsi, dating from AD 326, is a huge, still active temple complex, which was once the biggest monastery in Hangzhou, with thousands of monks. Its biggest Buddha, 19 m (over 60 ft) high, is made from 24 carved pieces of camphorwood.

Pagoda of the Six Harmonies

Liuheta, an octagonal pagoda south of Hangzhou, is a classic of 10th-century architecture. Made of brick and wood, it has 13 roofs one above the other, hung with dozens of bells, but only six storeys inside.

Ningbo

By rail or express highway, Ningbo is the major port of Zhejiang province, 150 km (94 miles) from Hangzhou. Although far smaller than Shanghai to the north across Hangzhou Bay, it can take bigger ships (up to 300,000 tonnes) and doesn't need constant dredging. It exported great quantities of silk, especially to Japan, from the 12th century onwards, and was one of the first Treaty Ports, opened to trade with the west, in 1842.

The city centre is some way inland, where the Yuyao and Yong rivers meet. The oldest part is around Moon Lake (*Yuehu*), where people still scrub clothes and children splash. Taifeng Pagoda, 60 m (almost 200 ft) high, is a landmark dating originally from the Tang dynasty but rebuilt in the 14th century; the view from its upper levels is worth the climb. Just to the west of Moon Lake is the Ming dynasty Tianyige Library, the oldest surviving depository of Buddhist books and manuscripts, dating from 1516. Its design, including a reservoir for use in case of fire, was so much admired that it was duplicated in seven imperial libraries built under the Qing dynasty. Some of the treasures are on show, and the adjoining garden is a haven of tranquillity.

A Ningbo speciality is the fresh seafood, particularly the crab dishes. Zhejiang province catches almost a third of China's haul of crustaceans, a staggering 3 million tonnes a year.

Mount Putuo

A 4-hour boat trip from Ningbo ferry terminal, Putuoshan is one of four mountains in China that are sacred to Buddism. A pretty little island 5 km (3 miles) long, it has been a place of pilgrimage since the 10th century, and the centre of the veneration of Guanyin, Goddess of Mercy. During the Cultural Revolution, many of the temples were damaged and the monks dispersed, but now hundreds of them are back and the buildings have been meticulously restored. To add to the temples, beautifully sited on hilltops, the shrines in caves and the countless carved Buddhas, the coastal scenery and the beaches are a bonus. Thousands, of Chinese tourists join the genuine pilgrims, and for those who want to stay longer than a day, there are hotels and guest-houses.

GUANGZHOU AND THE SOUTH

City Sights, Shamian Island, Foshan, Cuiheng,
Zhanjiang, Hainan Island, Guilin, Xiamen

When the first Qin emperor annexed the southern coast of China in the 3rd century BC, Guangzhou was already a significant port. By the 7th century AD it was trading with southeast Asia, India and beyond. Foreigners called it Canton, their version of the name of the province, Guangdong. The Portuguese arrived in the 16th century in search of trade, followed by the Dutch and British. They and other western nations set up "factories" (combining office, residential and storage facilities) along the waterfront, and exported tea, silk and porcelain. In exchange, Britain bartered increasing quantities of opium, even though its use was illegal in China. In 1839 the Chinese authorities seized and burned 20,000 chests of opium, and Britain retaliated by bombarding the port. It was an unequal contest, and in the peace treaty of 1842 China was forced to give Britain and other western powers a free hand in Guangzhou and other Treaty Ports. War broke out again in 1856, and Anglo-French forces occupied the city until 1861. At the same time the Taiping Rebellion, whose leader came from Guangzhou, stirred up further ferment.

Resentment against the distant and disastrous rule of the Qing emperors was focused into a revolutionary movement by the Guangdong-born Dr Sun Yatsen. An attempted uprising in 1911 failed, but it paved the way for the success of the revolution before the year was out. Later, Mao Zedong and Zhou Enlai cut their political teeth as followers of Dr Sun. When he died in 1925, Chiang Kaishek took over as leader. In 1927, a Communist attempt to set up a workers' commune in Guangzhou was bloodily crushed.

The Japanese bombed the city in 1937 and occupied it a year later. Although Chiang's Nationalists returned in 1945, their rule lasted only until the Communist victory of 1949. A huge trade fair instituted in 1957 restored Guangzhou's role as the main point of contact for foreign business. It has always been outward-looking; millions of overseas Chinese have their roots here, and have pumped in investment. Today the province of Guang-

Top: Guangzhou skyline.
Bottom: Taoist temple at Foshan.

dong continues as the power-house of Chinese trade, with 40 per cent of the total.

The city is more accessible than ever, only a short ride on a train or high-speed catamaran ferry up the Pearl River from Hong Kong. Five million people live in a quite compact space, and even by Chinese standards the streets are packed with pedestrians and traffic. You'd expect good Cantonese restaurants, and won't be disappointed, but the cosmopolitan population means the choice is much wider.

City Sights

Guangzhou spreads along the Pearl River, mainly on the north bank, 60 km (37 miles) from the sea.

Flower Pagoda

A central landmark is the 58-m (190-ft) Huata, also called the Ornate Pagoda, on the site of a 6th century predecessor built to house Buddhist relics brought from India. You can climb the stairs to the top—17 storeys, although from the outside there appear to be only nine. Liurong Temple at the foot of the pagoda has sadly lost the six banyan trees of its name.

A short walk to the west leads to Guangxiao Temple, the oldest Buddhist temple in the city, founded in the 5th century.

Huaisheng Mosque

Founded by Muslim traders, the mosque has what is claimed to be a 7th-century minaret. That would make it the world's oldest, apart from one in Mecca, but a more likely date is a century or two later. A tall, tapering round tower in Arabian style (unlike most minarets in China), it looks like a lighthouse, and doubled as one when it was first built and the Pearl River flowed nearer than it does now. The mosque's prayer hall and courtyard are purely Chinese in design. The worshippers are descendants of merchants who settled here throughout the Middle Ages, when there was substantial commerce with Indonesian and Arabian ports.

Around Yuexiu Park

The imposing, blue-tiled Sun Yatsen Memorial Hall, a 5000-seat auditorium, stands where the revolutionary leader proclaimed the republic in Guangzhong.

To the north in Yuexiu Park, Zhenhai tower, which formed part of the Ming city wall, now houses the Municipal Museum devoted to the history and art of the region. Also in the park, the Five Rams Statue depicts the animals which legend says carried five immortals down from heaven to found the city. Other versions of the story say they were goats, carrying rice to the starving.

Chen Family Temple

To the west of the city centre along Zhongshan Street, this temple was built by the rich Chen clan in the late 19th century. Amid a riot of colour, gilding and elaborate carving the buildings are now used for exhibitions of folk art, including the brilliant textiles of the tribes from southwest China.

Qingping Market

Filling a city block next to the river, this is the quintessential Chinese market on a grand scale: jostling crowds and hubbub, basic and exotic foods of every description sold from tiny stalls and big warehouses. Whole sections are given over to cage-birds, ornamental fish, flowers and pottery. Keep a close grip on your possessions, and if you can't stomach the idea of seeing owls behind bars, live snakes slit open or turtles, cats and chickens dispatched in a variety of ways, you may prefer to give the market a miss.

Revolutionary Memorials

City tours often visit sites connected with various stages of the Chinese revolution. The Museum of the Peasant Institute, east of the centre on Zhongshan Road, was a Communist Party training school where Mao Zedong and Zhou Enlai lectured in the 1920s.

Continuing on the same road, the Memorial to the Martyrs of the Guangzhou Rising stands in one of the city's most attractive parks. It honours more than 5000 who were killed when an attempted Communist insurrection was crushed by Nationalist forces in 1927.

On the northeastern outskirts in another park, the Mausoleum of the 72 Martyrs commemorates those who were executed after the failed uprising of 1911, only months before Sun Yatsen's successful revolution.

Shamian Island

The former British and French concessions shared this small island off the north bank of the Pearl River, opposite Qingping market. Merchants and bankers built attractive mansions, tennis courts and clubhouses, planted trees to give shade (some are now huge). At night the bridges were closed to keep out any Chinese, apart from servants. Some of the handsome buildings are now used by city bureaucrats or as consulates.

A river cruise is a relaxing way to see the waterfront and the perpetual motion of hundreds of ferries, sampans, motorized junks, coastal steamers and naval craft. On an island downriver, the Huangpu Military Academy was founded by Sun Yatsen. Mao 79

Zedong once attended a course there, under none other than Chiang Kaishek.

Foshan

A favourite excursion from Guangzhou heads for Foshan, 24 km (15 miles) to the southwest. The town is renowned for its crafts: silk, metalwork, woodcarving, ceramics and paper art. All of them and more have been put to use in beautifying the amazing Taoist Ancestral Temple, founded during the Northern Song dynasty between 1078 and 1085 and rebuilt in 1372 at the beginning of the Ming dynasty.

The Folk Art Studio specializes in elaborate paper-cutting, papier maché masks, lanterns and screen prints. The porcelain factory at nearby Shiwan is another stop on many itineraries; it turns out charming figures of animals, birds and characters from Chinese legend.

Cuiheng

Sun Yatsen was born in Cuiheng village, near the Pearl River estuary on the road to Macau. The family house, with high ceilings in the Portuguese colonial style, is a political shrine to the founder of the republic who practised as a doctor here. A museum of his career, with photographs and documents, stands in a memorial park.

Zhanjiang

Although it's in the same province as bustling Guangzhou, and the people speak the same dialect, Zhanjiang might as well be in another world. At the western end of Guangdong's subtropical coastline, it was closed to foreigners for many years. Now, they come for two main reasons: to take a ship to Hainan island, or to head for the offshore rigs drilling for oil and gas in the South China Sea.

Historically, Zhanjiang came to international attention in 1898 when France seized it and imposed a treaty on the weak Qing authorities in Beijing, to obtain a 99-year lease on the port and the nearby coast and islands. But it was overshadowed by the ports in French Indo-China (now Vietnam) and did not flourish. Japanese forces occupied Zhanjiang during World War II, and the French did not return.

The Port

The port today is busy with ferries and small craft serving the oil rigs. The city has some impressively wide boulevards but few notable buildings. Its prime monument is the 18th-century Upper Forest Temple, in the southeast suburb of Nan Liu. When the French invaded in 1898, local people gathered in front of the temple to coordinate resistance; after 1949, the Communists gave it the name: "Site of the Zhanjiang People's Anti-French Struggle".

Radiant Crag Lake

In the mountains 24 km (15 miles) southeast of Zhanjiang is an expanse of shimmering blue, ringed by purple cliffs rising sheer from the water's edge. Formed over a million years ago in the crater of an extinct volcano, Huguangyan caught the eye of a Song dynasty minister in the 12th century. He was so impressed by the reflections of light in the lake's surface that he carved the characters Radiant Crag Lake on a rock beside it.

At the water's edge, Surangama Temple was built by the monk Sun Zong in the Song dynasty and named after a Buddhist sutra. To the side, steps lead up to a natural cave surrounded by gardens and pavilions. Another Buddhist temple by the lake is known as the Convent of the White Robe.

Hainan Island

A tropical island off China's southern coast, Hainan was long regarded as a backwater, where disgraced imperial officials were sent as a punishment. Only during conflicts with Vietnam (the last as recently as 1978) did it occupy the minds of the central government. Forgotten no longer,

it is now China's largest Special Economic Zone, with abundant natural resources: offshore oil and gas deposits, iron ore and other minerals. Unfortunately, unregulated and wildly over-optimistic expansion, financial scandals and exploitation has left many projects half-finished and abandoned.

Until the 1950s, half the island's 34,000 sq km (13,000 sq miles) were covered by rainforest. Now the figure is less than a tenth; the rest has been cleared for rubber, banana, pineapple, coffee, coconut and sisal plantations and other agriculture, as well as housing. The population of 7 million, small by Chinese standards, includes 2 million minority Miao and Li peoples.

Hainan's palm-fringed white sand beaches, warm clear waters and gentler pace of life attract growing numbers of tourists, chiefly mainlanders and overseas Chinese. Coast roads built by the Japanese, who occupied Hainan from 1937 to 1945, have been upgraded, and augmented by highways linking all the main towns.

Haikou

On the north coast facing the mainland, the island's capital Haikou still has some pretty colonial-style buildings in the old quarter. The town's two notable monuments are some way from 81

The Ends of the Earth, a rock-strewn beach on Hainan Island.

the centre. The Tomb of Hairui, on the western outskirts, honours a revered Ming dynasty judge. Across town to the southeast is the 11th-century Temple to the Five Officials. These notables were Tang dynasty poets banished to the island. It also houses the city museum.

Crocodiles

China's biggest crocodile park is 20 km (12 miles) west of Haikou, not far from Horseshoe Crater, the relic of an extinct volcano.

Wenchang

The coconut groves of Wenchang on the northeast coast border fine sandy beaches. The town's chief claim to fame is as the birthplace of the Song sisters, who married Sun Yatsen and Chiang Kaishek.

Further down the coast, Xinglong Farm is known for its coffee and cacao, and the nearby hot springs resort.

South Coast

At the southern tip of Hainan, Sanya is a busy port and the main holiday centre. Dadonghai is the beach nearest town, with various watersports but crowded and not always clean. Yalong Bay, 8 km (5 miles) long, has the best hotels, while the so-called Ends of the Earth, 20 km (12 miles) west, is scattered with odd-shaped stones. The region specializes in cultivating pearls, a technique devised 1,000 years ago during the Song dynasty. Pearl farms welcome visitors.

The Highlands

The Tongshi highlands are home to the Li and Miao people. Tongshi, amid the remnants of the rainforest is the chief town, where they welcome tourists with undisguised commercialism, selling craftwork and trinkets and staging folklore shows.

To the northeast is Hainan's highest mountain, Wuzhishan. A steep scramble takes you to the 1,867 m (6,100 ft) summit in about 3 hours.

Guilin

For more than a thousand years, poets and painters have been inspired by Guilin's mirror-smooth rivers and tall pinnacles of rock; one Chinese saying calls them jade ribbons and emerald hairpins. Geologically, this an example of karst landscape, limestone eroded by rain, rivers and, in the distant past, submersion beneath the sea.

Guilin's fame has inevitably spread, bringing as great a concentration of tourists as you'll meet anywhere in China, many of them from Hong Kong or Taiwan. The local population includes many from minority tribal groups, such as the mainly Muslim Zhuang, and the Miao.

The City

Few historic buildings have survived in Guilin, since it was bombed and then captured by the Japanese in 1944, but the setting is spectacular. The Li river runs through the centre, the amazing hills start close by, and large parts have been designated as parks. A network of paths leads to a dozen caves, another karst phenomenon, to odd rock formations and ancient carvings.

Peaks and Caves

For a commanding view of the whole area, take a restful ride by chair lift to the top of Yaoshan. Or, more energetically, climb to the top of Fuboshan, passing hundreds of images of Buddha carved into the rock 1,000 years ago. At the base of the hill, right next to the river, Sword-Testing Stone is a stalactite formation resembling a column that has been cut through; legend says that a general passing this way 2000 years ago severed it with his blade.

Close by to the north, Diecaishan, Folded Brocade Hill, rises high above the city. Catch Cloud Pavilion on the 223-m (732-ft) summit provides a perfect panorama.

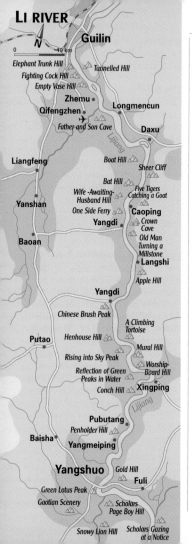

LI RIVER

N

0   40 km

Guilin

Elephant Trunk Hill
Tunnelled Hill
Fighting Cock Hill
Empty Vase Hill
Zhemu
Qifengzhen
Longmencun
Father-and-Son Cave
Daxu
Liangfeng
Boat Hill
Sheer Cliff
Bat Hill
Five Tigers
Catching a Goat
Wife-Awaiting-Husband Hill
Yanshan
One Side Ferry
Caoping
Yangdi
Crown Cave
Baoan
Old Man Turning a Millstone
Langshi
Apple Hill
Yangdi
Chinese Brush Peak
A Climbing Tortoise
Putao
Henhouse Hill
Mural Hill
Rising into Sky Peak
Worship-Board Hill
Reflection of Green Peaks in Water
Conch Hill
Xingping
Pubutang
Baisha
Penholder Hill
Yangmeiping
Yangshuo
Gold Hill
Fuli
Green Lotus Peak
Gaotian Scenery
Scholars Page Boy Hill
Snowy Lion Hill
Scholars Gazing at a Notice

Seven Star Park, on the east bank of the Li river facing the city, takes its name from seven pinnacles arranged in the shape of the Great Bear (or Big Dipper) constellation. The area is scattered with temples, pavilions, rock carvings and caves. The biggest, Seven Star Cave, has many striking formations. But if you are choosing just one cave to visit, the most spectacular is Reed Flute Cave on the northwestern outskirts of Guilin. Used as a bomb shelter in World War II, it is now a major attraction. Its forests of stalactites and stalagmites are given poetic names and bathed in coloured lights, but even this garish commercialism cannot blunt the impact of the huge "Crystal Palace".

The Li River Excursion

The highlight of a visit to Guilin is a trip along the meandering Li river (*Lijiang*). Every morning, a procession of big flat-bottomed boats like floating pavilions heads south on the 4¹/2-hour voyage downstream to Yangshuo, a distance of 83 km (52 miles). The gentle pace is ideally suited to the dreamy landscape, revealing one photogenic prospect after another as impossibly shaped peaks pass in endless succession. Maps provided on board helpfully number the main landmarks and their romantic names. Lunch is pre-

Along the banks of Banyan Tree River, a tributary of the Li.

pared in a cramped galley at the stern—some excuse for it being one of the duller meals you'll have in China. Just as fascinating is the scene along the shore: women laundering clothes, children splashing, water-buffalo drinking, farmers toiling in the rice-paddies. And on the water, small ferry boats run to and fro and you may see fisherfolk on bamboo rafts setting their trained cormorants to work; a ring round each bird's neck stops it swallowing the catch. (In Guilin itself, this is run as a tourist spectacle.)

At Yangshuo the throngs of passengers disembark, and the empty cruise boats turn to make the voyage home, much more slowly against the current. Hundreds of souvenir stalls fill every available spot along the river bank, but the rest of the town is quite charming. With plenty of restaurants and a scattering of hotels, it's a good base for exploring the area. However, most visitors simply transfer to buses for the return trip to Guilin, stopping at one or two riverside villages and picturesque spots along the way.

Xiamen

For millions of Chinese living overseas in Southeast Asia and beyond, Fujian province is what

85

they consider "home" and Xiamen (long known as Amoy) the port from which they or their ancestors sailed to seek their fortunes. Even today, descendants of the pioneers maintain the connection and favour Xiamen with investment.

The port, on an island off the rocky coast, began as a pirates' lair and centre for smuggling. To try to suppress these activities, a fort was built in the 14th century during the Ming dynasty. Until modern times, Xiamen remained quite isolated from the interior of China, cut off by the mountainous and thickly forested Fujian hinterland. Its people looked to the sea for trade, and established settlements all over the region, including Taiwan, 200 km (125 miles) away across the Formosa Strait. During the 17th century, after the fall of the Ming dynasty in mainland China, Ming loyalists led by Zheng Chenggong (known in the West as Koxinga) held out in Xiamen for many years, and then in Taiwan, having thrown the Dutch out of their settlements there.

Portuguese ships had arrived at Xiamen in the mid-16th century, followed by English, Dutch and Spanish, but the Chinese authorities severely restricted trade and foreigners were not allowed to settle. After the 1839–42 Opium War with Britain, Xiamen became one of the first five ports opened for foreign trade and residence, with tea as its most valuable export.

Like most of China's coast, Xiamen was occupied by the Japanese during World War II. When the war ended, the Europeans did not return, having agreed to cancel the "Unequal Treaties" forced on China in the 19th century. Communist forces took the port in 1949, but the Nationalists held (and still hold today) the nearby island of Jinmen (Quemoy), reinforced from their stronghold of Taiwan. Throughout the 1950s and 60s the two sides fought artillery duels, seriously hampering trade and development, but an unwritten ceasefire has held for many years now. Foreign tourism has been permitted since 1980, and Xiamen has been made a Special Economic Zone to encourage investment. Growth has been spectacular, with glittering high-rise buildings springing up in an imitation of Hong Kong. A causeway built in 1956 links the island by rail and road to the mainland, where development is also proceeding apace.

Xiamen is famous for its cooking, a variant of Fujianese, with emphasis naturally on seafoods. More surprisingly, it has three golf courses, one of them designed by Greg Norman.

The Port

The old port on Xiamen island is a maze of winding streets, with some charming 19th-century architecture. Running east from the docks, Zhongshan Road cuts through the centre; there's a lively market in Datong Road. In Zhongshan Park, among the lakes and pine trees, a huge marble monument honours Dr Sun Yat-sen (Zhongshan).

Gardens and Temples

On the eastern edge of the city, next to a reservoir, a monument to the Revolutionary Martyrs commemorates those who died in the wars that ended with the Communist victory in 1949. Beyond it is the Wanshi Park and Botanic Garden, renowned for its thousands of species of tropical and sub-tropical plants, and its picturesque rocks, some of them inscribed with Chinese characters singing the praises of the scenery.

This part of the island is dotted with Buddhist temples. At the Tianjie temple, the monks used to strike a bell at dawn which echoed through the hills. A highlight of any visit to Xiamen is the Nanputuo temple, built over 1000 years ago on the slopes to the south of Wanshi. It is still a working Buddhist centre, with a renowned vegetarian restaurant. Dabeidian, the Hall of Great Compassion, was originally a wooden structure, but after a fire in the 1930s it was rebuilt in concrete, to the same design. Not far away is Xiamen University, founded with the help of contributions from overseas Chinese.

Gulangyu

The foreign residents of Xiamen used to live on the hilly little island of Gulangyu, a ferry ride across the harbour. It remains a delightful retreat, garlanded with flowers all the year round. As you climb its slopes, you'll see traces of the colonial past all around, in the gracious old mansions—some crumbling, some restored—and former consulates. Sunlight Cliff (*Riguangyan*), the highest point at 90 m (300 ft), commands superb views of Gulangyu, Xiamen and its harbour, the mainland and the sea. The Ming general Koxinga stationed his troops on the hill, and traces of his defences can still be seen.

On the southern slopes, Shuzhuang Gardens use the natural contours in a miniature landscape that includes 44 bridges and an artificial hill with caves hollowed into it. The Koxinga Memorial Hall has relics of the general, including his jade belt, and an exhibition about his victory over the Dutch. At the southeastern tip of Gulangyu a massive stone statue standing high on a rock gazes out to sea, towards Taiwan.

HONG KONG

Hong Kong Island, Kowloon, New Territories, Lantau, Cheung Chau, Lamma

If Hong Kong were a separate nation, it would rank among the world's top ten for trade. The barren island that Britain acquired in 1841 after the first Opium War has come a long way. The Kowloon peninsula on the mainland was added to the colony in 1860, following a second war. Then in 1898 China gave Britain a 99-year lease on the New Territories and 235 offshore islands, multiplying the total area by ten to over 1000 sq km (400 sq miles). As a free port, Hong Kong quickly took over much of southern China's import and export trade. People poured in from neighbouring Guangdong province to work, and a new wave of immigrants was generated by every upheaval in China: the 1911 revolution, the civil wars, the Japanese invasion. In December 1941, a few hours after the attack on Pearl Harbor, Japanese forces launched an assault on Hong Kong. The colony surrendered on Christmas Day, beginning $3^{1}/_{2}$ years of privation and ill-treatment. Many Chinese were deported: the population fell from 1.5 million to only half a million.

After the war, normal service slowly resumed. The Communist triumph in 1949 brought a rush of refugees. In making a new life for themselves, setting up workshops and factories, they built the future prosperity of Hong Kong. The influx continued, mainly of the young and poor, and construction of housing became the major industry. To stem the flow, the frontier was closed in 1962; illegal arrivals risked deportation back to the People's Republic.

China could have choked Hong Kong's economy at any time by banning trade, but chose not to. On the contrary, the colony became its biggest trading partner, and the new city of Shenzen was built next to the border to take advantage.

Handover

With the clock ticking towards 1997, Britain and China agreed on terms for the return not only of the leased territories but the whole of the colony. Seeing Hong Kong as a catalyst for modernizing the mainland's economy, the pragmatic Deng Xiaoping guaranteed that Hong Kong would remain a capitalist enclave, with its own currency and laws, free speech and travel. "One country, two systems" was the promise, and so far it has been kept.

Growth faltered during the Asian financial crisis of 1998 but soon resumed. The population, now approaching 7 million, is expected to reach 10 million by the year 2015. New land is constantly being won from the sea; it may not be long before Hong Kong Island is an island no more. New lines are planned for the mass transit rail system, or MTR, and the Kowloon-Canton Railway, to try to curb the inexorable rise in road traffic and congestion.

Star Attraction

Road tunnels and the MTR dive beneath the harbour, but whether you are staying in Kowloon or on the island, there's no better introduction than to take the Star Ferry between the two. For a minimal fare you get a taste of the pace of life as you're propelled by a crowd of commuters on to the double-decker waterbus. Bells clang, the gangplank is raised, the sailors cast off and you head out across the harbour through

swarms of other craft of every size and description. The views of the island, glittering skyscrapers massed on its waterfront and up the hillsides, and at night of the lights, are superb.

Hong Kong Island

The first British settlement, on the north coast of the island, grew into today's glittering city. They called it Victoria, a name not much used now, although the sheltered waters of the strait between the island and Kowloon on the mainland are still sometimes known as Victoria Harbour.

Central

The prosaically named heart of the city extends from the Star Ferry terminal both ways along the shoreline (on land won from the sea) and up the gentle slopes behind. Hemmed in by skyscrapers, the open spaces of Statue Square and Chater Garden offer a restful break sitting on the park

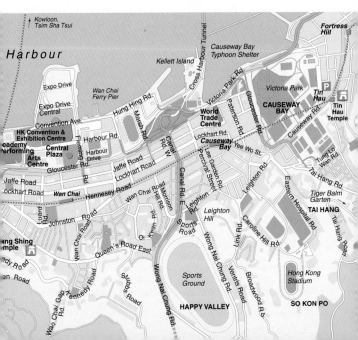

Everyone climbs to Victoria Peak for a sky-high view.

benches in the shade of trees—unless it's Sunday, when hundreds of Filipino maids gather here on their day off for a chat and a picnic. The south side of the square is dominated by the huge steel-and-glass Hongkong and Shanghai Bank headquarters, designed by Sir Norman Foster. Nearby to the east is the even taller blue glass tower of the rival Bank of China, by the Chinese-American architect I.M. Pei.

For a ride on a relic, board one of the double-decker trams that rattle along Des Voeux Road; the venerable vehicles are a bizarre contrast to the dot.com ads emblazoned on their sides. Also sur-viving among the modernity, behind the banking giants, are the mid-19th century St John's Anglican Cathedral and the old Government House, residence of British governors from 1855 to 1997. On the hill above, the Zoological and Botanical Gardens attract the locals for their early morning *tai chi* exercises. The caged birds and animals here are mainly native to south China. The larger Hong Kong Park behind the Bank of China is notable for its big walk-through aviary.

The Peak

Head up Garden Road from the Bank of China tower and you'll

come to the terminus of the Peak Tram, a funicular railway dating from 1888 (but totally rebuilt) that climbs to the highest point of the island. The ride up passes gradually more affluent apartments and then luxurious villas—it's cool to live as high as you can afford. The Peak itself, 550 m (1,805 ft) high, has unfortunately been disfigured by an ugly concrete shopping and entertainment complex, but the view from the top is worth the trip. If you want to take photographs, remember that the city below is north-facing and loses the sun quite early. There's also a road to the top, and a bus; it's a tough walk up (exercise fanatics love to run it) and a pleasant stroll down.

Central West

West of the Star Ferry pier is the island's main transport interchange, for the new railway to Chep Lap Kok airport, the MTR and buses. The streets around here are not meant for strolling; pedestrians are funnelled into overhead walkways that lead direct to office towers and shopping centres.

Just inland past De Voeux Road begins the world's longest chain of escalators and moving walkways, climbing the slopes to the residential Mid Levels. Until 10 a.m. it runs downhill, bringing commuters and servants on their way to the shops. The rest of the day it goes up. There's a break in the system at Hollywood Road, known for its antique shops, some of them displaying their treasures like museum galleries. For more modest prices look at the market stalls in the side alleys.

Along Hollywood Road to the west is Hong Kong's oldest temple, Man Mo, where the incense smoke is often thick enough to force you back, gasping for air. At the next crossing, Ladder Street is one of many streets so steep that they turn into flights of steps.

East of Central

The shoreline arcs east from Central through Wanchai, past the giant exhibition centre on its artificial headland. A low-life strip until the 1980s, Wanchai still has plenty of bars and restaurants, but the power of money has overshadowed them with a wall of office towers. Causeway Bay, more land than water since most was infilled, has the best shopping and the biggest selection of eating places on the island.

Inland, at Happy Valley racetrack, Hong Kong's inveterate gamblers bet an annual 90 *billion* dollars on the horses. Race meetings take place on Wednesdays and Saturdays from September to June.

Round the Island

On the deeply indented south coast, Aberdeen harbour is crowded with sampans and junks, but far fewer than there once were. Since a fatal fire swept through the tightly packed craft, most of the boat-dwellers have been moved ashore to live in huge apartment buildings. You can take a sampan trip past the old houseboats that remain, or out to one of the floating restaurants, decked out like an imperial palace.

East of Aberdeen, Ocean Park is a multi-theme attraction, with thrilling rollercoasters, boat rides, huge aquariums, performing dolphins and seals. A long cable-car system climbs up to a high headland, and down again to The Middle Kingdom, a living lesson in Chinese history, architecture, arts and crafts. The separate Waterworld has a wave pool and slides.

Sand imported from the Philippines has improved the beaches at Deep Water Bay and Repulse Bay, packed with sunbathers in summer. Swimmers are protected by shark-proof nets. Stanley, on the next long finger of land, has a popular market selling clothing, crafts and souvenirs.

Kowloon

The Star ferries and cruise ships dock at the end of Kowloon peninsula, the shopping and hotel district called Tsimshatsui. As you head away from the pier, on your right is the futuristic Hong Kong Cultural Centre with its windowless façade and curving roof. It houses art galleries, a concert hall, and the Museum of Art, which showcases fine examples of ancient Chinese art from the Han to the Ming and Qing dynasties, as well as international works. Nearby is the Space Museum and a planetarium, called the Space Theatre, with daily Omnimax screenings and Sky shows.

Nathan Road, the wide tree-lined avenue from south to north right through Kowloon, was the idea of Sir Matthew Nathan, governor from 1904 to 1907. Until the 1960s it was a quiet suburban road; now the southern end is consumers' paradise.

Passing Kowloon Mosque (closed to non-believers), Nathan Road borders the green spaces of Kowloon Park, once the site of a Qing dynasty fort. The Museum of History on the corner of Austin and Chatham Road covers the region's past using the latest display techniques.

From the Kowloon-Canton (Guangzhou) Railway terminus, east of Tsimshatsui, trains serve the New Territories and, for those with a visa, Guangzhou.

Kai Tak was Hong Kong's airport until 1998. Generations of

Double-deckers rattle through a jungle of signs entreating you to buy, buy, buy.

travellers recall swooping in low over the rooftops of Kowloon, looking into top floor apartments, and landing on a runway sticking out into the sea with minimal margins for error. Then overnight all operations moved to the new Chep Lap Kok airport off Lantau island.

In North Kowloon, the Sung Dynasty Village is a reproduction 1000-year old village with people in period costume, working on crafts and giving street performances.

The New Territories
The name of Boundary Street recalls the days before Britain leased the New Territories in 1898. You won't notice any sudden change, but a tour of the "NT" is full of variety and some surprises. Parts are highly industrialized and densely populated; Tsuen Wan just west of Kowloon is a city of a million people with one of the world's biggest container ports. But most of the area is still rural, with traditional agriculture, and the coastline is wonderfully scenic.

Shatin
A huge city in its own right, Shatin is known for its race track, bigger and far more luxurious than the island's Happy Valley. 95

Its spacious facilities include a swimming pool—for the horses. High on a hill to the west is the Ten Thousand Buddha Monastery. For once, the name is not an exaggeration: there are more than ten thousand! The way up involves climbing hundreds of steps, or taking the escalator.

Kat Hing Wai

The genuine, walled and moated village of Kat Hing Wai (or Kam Tin) dates from the 17th century. It was built by Hakka people who had migrated south from the Yangtze valley. Their descendants still live here; the older women wear flat straw hats with black cloth flaps round the brim.

Mai Po Marshes

In the northwest near the border with Guangdong province, fish ponds line the muddy sea shore. Inland on the wetlands are more fish and duck farms, and a nature reserve where more than 250 species of resident and migrating birds have been recorded.

Lantau

By far the biggest of the outer islands, Lantau remains largely rural, with a population of only about 40,000. Until recently it never had a reliable water supply, and could only be reached by an hour's ferry trip. Now bridges carry road and rail links to the island on their way to Chep Lap Kok, the new Hong Kong International Airport, and at least in the northeast corner of Lantau the days of peace and quiet are over. A Disneyland opened there in 2005. A mountain was levelled and dumped in the sea to create the airport, an artificial island, 5 km (3 miles) long. Work started long before the territory was due to return to China, and the cost became a bone of contention, Chinese ministers complaining that Britain was emptying the treasury before the handover.

Cheung Chau

Just off the south coast of Lantau and an hour's trip from Central or Kowloon, Cheung Chau was a fishing village and base for smugglers before the British came to Hong Kong. The little dumb-bell shaped island is packed with traditional shops and houses, a few temples, plenty of restaurants—and people, 40,000 of them.

Lamma

A short trip from Aberdeen, or a longer one from Central, Lamma makes a perfect getaway spot. Ferries serve the only two villages, Yung Shue Wan and Sok Kwu Wan, both with restaurants and separated by a 40-minute walk. There are no roads, and no cars. The power station at the west end strikes an incongruous note.

MACAU
The City, The Islands

A Portuguese colony since the middle of the 16th century, Macau was returned to China at the end of 1999. The change was barely noticed; nothing had happened there for years without Chinese approval. China could have repossessed the tiny enclave at any time but found it a convenient gateway. There's still a checkpoint at the old border; like Hong Kong, the territory now has the status of a Special Administrative Region, with its own currency, the *pataca*.

The Portuguese explorer Jorge Alvares reached the south China coast in 1513. With the agreement of local mandarins, Portuguese merchants soon set up trading posts in several ports, including the peninsula they called A-Ma Gao (the Bay of the Sea Goddess A-Ma), or Macau. Word came from the Ming emperor in Beijing that they would be tolerated, but only in one settlement. By 1557, all European traders were concentrated at Macau, which became China's main opening to the west for 100 years. Missionaries hoping to spread the Christian message made it their base, setting up the first western college in the Far East. European rivals were envious of Portugal's favoured status; the Dutch tried to capture Macau in 1622 but were beaten off.

Gradually, limited trade with other Chinese ports was permitted, and when Britain acquired Hong Kong in the 1840s, Macau was sidelined. That was when it was decided to cash in on the Chinese love of gambling (illegal in China) and open a casino, the first of many. They have been the territory's chief source of income ever since. They're open 24 hours a day, with the usual roulette, blackjack and thousands of slot machines, plus the local favourites *fantan* and *daisiu* ("big and small"), played with three dice.

Portuguese neutrality during World War II made Macau a magnet for refugees and a stamping ground for spies. After the war it picked up some business on the back of Hong Kong's booming prosperity. Now, Macau has its own airport, the runway dramatically sited on an artificial island.

The peninsula, two islands linked to it by bridges and causeways, plus some land won from the sea, together add up to only 23 sq km (9 sq miles). Into this space are crammed almost half a million people, but compared to Hong Kong it doesn't seem crowded. Ferries and jetfoils from Hong Kong pass under the long

Friendship Bridge to land at a terminal on the east side of the peninsula. Those from Guangzhou dock on the west side.

The City

The peninsula is shaped like a pointed shoe, with the border at the northern "ankle" end. The first settlement was at the toe, guarded by the 17th-century Barra fortress that is now the superb setting for a luxury hotel. On the west side, the colourful Taoist A-Ma Temple to the goddess of the sea was probably here before the Portuguese. The Maritime Museum tells the story of Chinese as well as Portuguese voyages of exploration, and next to it at Pier No 1 you can take a short cruise around the harbour.

On the east of the peninsula, Avenida da Praia Grande used to run along the seafront, but the bay has been enclosed by causeways to form a lake—the first step in creating more dry land. Largo do Senado (Senate Square) is the heart of the city, paved in a wavy mosaic pattern and surrounded by classical Portuguese buildings. At the southern end is the historic Leal Senado (the "Loyal Senate"), its courtyard lined with blue-and-white *azulejos* (tiles). The baroque São Domingos cathedral stands at the other end of the square.

The Saint Paul (*São Paulo*) façade somehow manages to look like a Chinese ceremonial gate, as well as the west front of a baroque church, which is what it was (originally called the Church of the Mother of God). Jesuit priests commissioned Chinese and Japanese craftsmen to work on the building, completed in 1602. In 1835, it was destroyed by fire, leaving only this imposing remnant. Behind it are the foundations, a crypt with relics of Christian martyrs and a museum of religious art.

The nearby Museum of Macau traces the history of the city and its unique way of life, while a walk on the 17th-century ramparts of the Monte fortress gives the best views over the whole area.

Portugal's national poet, Luis de Camões (1524–80) was exiled to the colonies after unwisely writing love poems to a lady on whom the king also had his eye. On the north side of the square named after him, Jardim Camões is a pretty, tree-shaded park.

To the east is the Old Protestant Cemetery, with many evocative gravestones of Europeans who died, mostly young, in Macau in the 18th and 19th centuries.

The Islands

Taipa and Coloane used to be quiet, remote and almost rural retreats from the city. Now two bridges link Taipa to the peninsula, and the airport has been built at the eastern end of the island. With the University of Macau, international hotels and industrial development, Taipa is becoming as busy as the mainland. It is joined to Coloane by two causeways, and land hunger is such that the space between them has been filled in to create one island. So far, Coloane remains green and pleasant, with Macau's best beaches on the south shore. The St Francis Xavier chapel preserves an elbow bone of the travelling saint, who came to this coast in 1549 on his way to Japan.

The poignant remains of Saint Paul's church.

101

Cultural Notes

Jade

For over 6000 years, jade has been esteemed in China for its unique properties of translucence, hardness and strange tactile quality. Seen as indestructible, it was used in rituals in life and then buried with the dead in the belief that it had the power to protect the body in the afterlife. In Han dynasty royal burials in the 2nd century BC, the whole body was covered by a suit made of more than 2000 delicately carved slices of jade. Tang era court officials wore belts of gold and jade, the number of pieces denoting their rank.

The word jade covers two distinct minerals, nephrite and jadeite, both of them complex silicates. As well as the green that takes its name from jade, it comes in shades of ivory, pink and yellow, coloured by traces of iron, manganese and other metals. Nephrite, the form so prized in ancient China, has a waxy appearance and is remarkably tough and difficult to break. Jadeite looks more glass-like and is even harder. It came much later to China from Burma, in the 18th century, but didn't catch on until the Empress Cixi acquired a taste for the finest pieces.

The hardness (6 to 7 on the Mohs scale; diamond being 10) makes jade exceptionally difficult to work. It cannot be carved, but has to be cut, ground and drilled with diamond and quartz tools, a lengthy and painstaking process. The lure of jade endures: ordinary Chinese wear simple pieces of jade jewellery for its protective powers, while international collectors pay millions of dollars for famous art treasures.

Language

If you include all the dialects, Chinese is the most widely used language on earth. In its written form it is probably also the one that has changed least in the last 2000 years, in fact since lists of characters were engraved in stone. The spoken variations such as Cantonese and Shanghainese are utterly different and mutually incomprehensible, but two factors unite the people that use them and make the country work. First, although the sounds are so different, the written characters are practically the same. Secondly, there's a national language, Mandarin, adapted from that used in educated circles in Beijing; it's taught in schools, used in the media and is the official language of Taiwan.

The characters that make up the written language are not letters or words but pictograms, made up of from one to twenty or more elements (such as fire, roof, air, man, stone). They represent ideas or concepts, both simple and subtle. When they are turned into speech, each character equals one single syllable which, notoriously, can mean several quite different things. As a further refinement, each syllable when spoken is given one of four "tones" (rising, falling, down and up and flat) which completely change the meaning.

There are said to be 50,000 characters, of which 10,000 are in use. A high-school student is expected to know 6,000. A foreigner studying Chinese would need to memorize 400 basic characters before beginning to read very simple texts.

Pinyin is a written phonetic system, rendering the sounds of Mandarin in Roman (western) script to make it easier to learn. But unless the tones are marked over the letters and correctly used, it is not much help in making yourself understood. It may all sound rather daunting, but bear in mind that millions of Chinese children take it in their stride. Start by the phrases for Hello, Please, Thank You, How much? Or even I don't understand; the response is usually rewarding and you'll soon find you want to learn more.

Opera

A vivid spectacle of gorgeous costumes, rainbow-coloured make-up, dance, acrobatics, battle scenes and melodrama, Chinese opera is unique. If the opening music sounds to your western ears like five different percussion bands tuning up, just wait for the singers' falsetto tones. The plots may seem impenetrable, but they are actually quite simple: good against evil; boy meets girl, loses girl, finds girl again, happy ever after.

Facial make-up proclaims character—red for honest leaders, black for brave soldiers, green for evil spirits, multi-coloured for the baddies. There are few stage

103

props; actors show by gestures when they are opening a door, or entering a house (taking a high step over an imaginary threshold). A man with a lantern means it's night; four men carrying flags represent a whole army. Costumes are colour-coded, with yellow robes for an emperor, green for good nobles, crimson for traitors and barbarian generals. It is all highly stylized, emphatic and loud, supposedly because it began in tea-rooms where audiences paid little attention unless their senses were assaulted. If you don't fancy a whole performance, try one of the packages which include a short sample of opera as part of an evening city tour.

Religion

From 1949, when the People's Republic was proclaimed, religious practice was discouraged. A few years later, during the Cultural Revolution, it was viciously suppressed. Taoist temples, Confucian halls and Buddhist temples and monasteries were attacked by fanatical Red Guards; many were burned to the ground; Buddhist monks were beaten or even killed. Mosques did not escape damage, and most churches were wrecked, closed or turned to secular use—Chinese Christians were particularly persecuted. Tens of thousands of ancient and beautiful buildings were destroyed, together with their treasures, although a

few were protected on orders from the top.

Today, the official view seems to be that people's religious beliefs are their own affair, provided they don't force them on others or get mixed up with politics. Many places of worship have reopened; Buddhist and Taoist temples are busy again, not just with the older generation but many young people, too.

Silk

According to legend, a silkworm cocoon fell into an empress's cup of tea and the thread began to unwind. No matter how the discovery was made, silk fabric has been produced in China for at least 4000 years. When it reached the west by way of the Silk Road, it provoked amazement. Some thought it was woven from cobwebs, others that the thread grew on trees.

The first stage of silk production, from egg to cocoon, is still largely a cottage industry. Many farmers grow a few mulberry trees to feed the silkworms which are hatched in two batches, spring and autumn, from eggs provided by the local factory.

Silk moths lay about 400 eggs, which take 12 days to hatch; the old method of using human body heat has been superseded by artificial incubators. The worm, or caterpillar, grows to 6 cm (2.4 in)

in 30 days, feeding on mulberry leaves in the process and shedding its skin four times. It then takes two days to wrap itself in a cocoon formed from a continuous thread of silk, averaging over 1100 m (1200 yd) in length. Afterwards, the shrunken worm turns into a pupa which, if it were left alone, would turn into a moth, mate, lay eggs if female, and die. To prevent this, the cocoons are steamed or baked. At the factory, they are sorted; broken ones are discarded and double cocoons (made by two worms) set to one side.

After boiling to remove gelatin, they are mounted in groups of eight on a frame, and sharp-eyed women locate the end of each one with a brush. The eight filaments are then wound off the cocoons and spun—twisted together—into a single thread. Dried and re-wound onto larger reels, the silk is then ready for weaving.

The double cocoons cannot be unwound, the two filaments being hopelessly tangled. They are stretched out into sheets and used in multiple layers as the filling for luxurious quilted bedcovers.

Much of the fabric you'll see labelled as silk in street markets is not the real thing, but an artificial fibre or a mixture. Experts can tell by the feel, and by burning a tiny piece; the smell and the form of the ash are unmistakeable.

Shopping

A vast range of traditional crafts, armies of skilled workers to produce them, an unrivalled instinct for commerce and the sheer need to earn a living all combine to make China the world's biggest emporium. Faced with souvenir shops at every tourist attraction, market stalls on every street, department stores in every city and more shops back at the hotel, even the most dedicated shopper may beg for mercy.

Organized tours always include visits to factories and workshops producing carpets, silk, porcelain, embroideries, jewellery or jade carvings, and naturally there's a chance to buy. Some of the items on sale will be the same everywhere you go, but others will be local products which you may never see again. So if you are really attracted to a particular cloisonné pot, a painting or some freshwater pearls, it could be a good idea to buy while you have the chance.

Antiques and Reproductions

Fascinating though it is to pick your way through the heaps of bygones on offer all over China, you are unlikely to find any undiscovered treasures. Many experts have come this way before you, including local collectors and dealers who are fully informed about world prices. Note that strictly speaking, antiques are anything over 100 years old, semi-antiques over 50 years old.

The Chinese authorities prohibit the export of cultural relics, apart from fairly modern and commonplace items which are marked with special seals. Keep all your receipts in case of difficulties with customs.

Hong Kong is a freer market, with many dealers whose stocks are of museum quality, beautifully displayed and lit. They will provide certificates of authenticity, and since their business depends on their reputation, you should get what you pay for.

Arts and Crafts

The choice is bewildering, from a disposable paper fan to a priceless jade figure. It easy to be enticed into making so many purchases that you end up having to buy another suitcase. Traditional paintings of landscapes, birds and animals are usually mounted as scrolls, so they can simply be rolled up and carried, and red paper lanterns can fit into a long tube. There is similarly no problem packing silks or brocades, either made up into clothing or as lengths of fabric.

If you buy fragile items such as porcelain, the sales staff will pack them in padded boxes ready to travel.

Carpets

By western standards, carpets are attractive and temptingly priced, and it's intriguing to see them being made, generally by young women or teenage girls. Very fine silk carpets take the longest time: the knots are so tiny. A quite small silk carpet 3 m long and 80 cm wide may take one girl two years to finish (being too narrow for more than one to work on).

At the other end of the scale are the coarser but colourful wool carpets and kilims from Xinjiang, made by central Asian ethnic groups such as the Uzbeks and Uighurs.

Pearls and Gems

The Chinese are highly skilled at cultivating pearls, using freshwater mussels and clams as hosts; some of the bigger mollusks can grow 20 or more pearls at the same time. The large, perfect specimens are set in expensive jewellery, but strings of the rougher, uneven pearls are charming and cost absurdly little.

BARGAINING

In the Friendship Stores run for visitors, in big shops, department stores and factory outlets, prices are fixed. Elsewhere, you can bargain, or at least ask for a discount. Of course, it's easier if you have some idea of the going rate, so a prior visit to the fixed-price stores can help. A few suggestions: don't appear too keen to buy; wait for the vendor to name a price (or write it down), then offer much less; let the vendor move towards your price, making only small concessions yourself; and don't hesitate to walk away.

You are certain to be approached by hawkers, especially at the entrances to tourist sites—they are not normally permitted inside. If you are not interested in buying, the best way to deal with them is to ignore them—avoid eye contact! Some are adept at applying moral pressure, for example by quickly making a paper-cut of your profile.

In Hong Kong, jewellery sells at favourable prices. But seek a reputable dealer. Diamons are said to cost about ten per cent less than elsewhere.

Souvenirs
You probably won't want to invest in your own full-size terra-cotta warrior, but you'll see miniature versions, models of the Qin emperor's bronze chariots, and even playing cards with images of the figures.

You might like to have your own name-seal, or "chop", used with an ink-pad (always red) to put the Chinese equivalent of a signature on documents. Street-corner chop-makers will work out a Chinese version of your name, or use the western original if you prefer, and carve it into a little block of bamboo, plastic or soapstone.

On backstreet pushcarts you may find old Chinese coins, bird cages, tiny scales in flat boxes, and attractive snuff bootles.

If you acquire a taste for black, green, white, scented or semi-fermented tea, take some home. The markets offer an endless variety of spices and herbs, dried roots and strange-looking bits of twig. Look for delicious dried fruits such as kumquats, apricots and wild cherries.

If you need a cap, you'll find plenty of choice at Xi'an.

Dining Out

Each region has its own special dishes, so a tour of China is a culinary adventure. Whenever you can, let a local expert order for you. Every meal should balance flavours, textures and colours, creating a feast for your eyes as well as a treat for your taste buds.

A great advantage of travelling with a group is that you can eat lunch and dinner in a very Chinese way. There's no need to order; a wide variety of dishes will be brought to the table and the diners help themselves. If the server doesn't say what each dish is, ask (there will usually be someone who can tell you, in English). The dishes generally arrive in quick succession, covering the surface of the table, or the conveniently revolving "lazy susan" in the centre.

Regional Styles

Moving from one province to another, you'll notice how cooking methods and ingredients vary, depending on the local products. The coastal provinces use plenty of fish and shellfish; rice is the staple in the warm, wet south, while wheat and maize (corn) are commoner in the north and northwest, where the harsher climate does not suit rice. Especially in the past, food in these areas had

to be preserved through the winter by salting, pickling, drying or smoking. To brighten up what might have been a repetitive diet, liberal use was made of fiery spices, and they still feature in many dishes.

Mildly flavoured but colourful and inventive Cantonese (Guangdong) cuisine is well known in the west, though often in a debased form. On its home territory, and in neighbouring Hong Kong, it's at its best, with stir-fried dishes, lightly cooked vegetables, chicken marinated in ginger and rice wine, pigeon, roast suckling pig, sweet-and-sour pork or prawns, and steamed rice as the staple starch. Costly delicacies which turn up on Cantonese menus include shark's fin, boiled and shredded and served alone or in a soup, and bird's nest, the translucent threads of sea swifts' nests served in a soup or with chicken.

Fuzhou cooking, from Fujian province, features even more 109

seafood than Cantonese, subtle flavours, many fresh herbs and a variety of soups. Hainan Island is famous for its chicken, fattened up on rice, sweet potato and coconut. It is stuffed with ginger, boiled and served with garlic-flavoured rice and a sauce made with chillies and fresh limes.

Shanghai has taken the dishes of surrounding provinces and refined them into a rich and varied cuisine, rather heavier and oilier than the southern coastal styles. It's famous for freshwater crabs, fried eel, fried noodles with shrimp, and braised or stewed seafoods in dark soy sauce with generous flavourings of spices and herbs.

Far from the sea and the rice-growing areas, the western provinces are noted for liberal use of spices. Sichuan (Szechuan) food tends to fire-bomb your taste buds with red-hot chillies and lip-numbing wild pepper, as in diced chicken with pepper, or hot and sour soup. But it also employs the softer flavours of ginger, garlic and fennel seed. Look out for Sichuan smoked duck, impregnated with the scents of smouldering tea leaves and exotic woods. Hunanese cooking is similar but a little less spicy and oily.

Noodles hung up to dry outside a factory in downtown Macau.

Each northern province has its own traditions, but as the capital, Beijing gets the most attention. Wheat and corn are the local cereal crops, so noodles, buns and dumplings are staples. Meats are pan-fried, barbecued or stewed. Beijing is the logical place to try Peking Duck: some famous restaurants there serve very little else, and display photographs of the world leaders who have dined in their establishment. Dipped in a sweet syrup, dried and roasted to a golden brown, the duck is carved in a special way, into 108 pieces (one of China's famous lucky numbers!). Diners take thin slices of the meat and tasty skin, add some green spring onions and sweet bean sauce, wrap it all in paper-thin pancakes and eat.

Dim sum

A southern custom that has spread all over China, dim sum (*dianxin* in Mandarin) is a late breakfast or early lunch consisting of a range of snacks, wheeled round the dining room so you can take your pick. Prawn and pork dumplings steamed in bamboo baskets, fried or steamed savoury buns, spring rolls, spare ribs, and a dozen other ingenious morsels can add up to a filling meal, with a few miniature desserts such as sago puddings and custard tarts. All this is washed down with co-pious quantities of tea.

Banquets

Birthdays, weddings and other celebrations are marked by a banquet, and the hospitality shown to visiting groups usually includes a welcome or farewell banquet, or both. Ten, twelve or more courses are served, in rapid succession, so it's best to take a small portion of each dish as it is offered. Don't be surprised if they come in an unfamiliar order: sweet before savoury; soup towards the end; and just when you thought it was all over, a large steamed fish. And don't ask for a bowl of rice; it often doesn't figure on the menu, being considered too mundane for a special occasion.

ETIQUETTE

Use the serving spoons provided, not your own chopsticks, to take food from serving dishes. It is considered impolite to take the last morsel from a plate; that implies that there was not enough to eat. Slurping soup is perfectly acceptable, in fact it's expected. So is picking up your rice bowl and pushing the rice into your mouth with the chopsticks.

It is not the custom to linger at the end of a meal. As soon as they have finished, Chinese diners are ready to get up and go, and you're supposed to do the same.

Oddities

Some visitors worry that they'll be served exotic and endangered species of wildlife, or perhaps something they'd rather not eat, such as cat, dog, snake or bamboo rat. They can rest assured that this is unlikely. Although such things are highly esteemed and certainly available (especially in southwestern China), they are generally expensive, and not to be wasted on ignorant foreigners unaware of the supposed health benefits of consuming them. Not quite in this category, in northern China you may be offered donkey, served in thin slices, like cold salt beef.

Vegetarian Dishes

In a country with so many Buddhists, you can naturally find vegetarian dishes, although some Buddhists do eat meat. The problem is to determine which dishes actually *are* vegetarian. Some cooks can't seem to resist adding a bit of pork to the cabbage or beans. And curiously, a great deal of skill is devoted to creating exact imitations of roast pork, duck, chicken, ham and sausage out of bean curd skin, gluten and mushrooms. Some Buddhist monasteries have public restaurants where the food is sure to be meat-free but fairly mild in flavour, as they don't spice the dishes with garlic, ginger or spring onions, considering them to be too stimulating.

Other Options

As if all the variations of Chinese cooking were not enough, you'll find many more choices. Many big hotels have an Italian restaurant; other popular alternatives are Japanese, Thai and US-style steak houses. And there's no escaping familiar fast-food—famous-name fried chicken and hamburger outlets are popping up all over the cities.

Breakfast

Chinese people start the day with something bland and simple: thin rice porridge or noodle soup, perhaps with fried dough or a bun. On the way to work, they may pick up a baked sweet potato or grilled sweetcorn. Hotels used by westerners provide something more substantial, usually a buffet with fruits, juices, cereals and hot dishes such as scrambled egg and bacon. Typical Chinese choices are included too, so you'll have a chance to try them.

Timing

Local people eat early: around 6 or 7 a.m. for breakfast, 11 a.m. to noon for lunch and as early as 5 p.m. for dinner. Hotels adapt to foreign habits but you may still find that breakfast is over by 9 a.m., lunch by 1 p.m., and staff

Counting the morning's takings in a village market near Guilin.

pointedly clearing up for the night by 8 p.m.

Drinks

Tea is omnipresent, and taken without milk or sugar. A big pot of basic black tea is served with most meals, starting out hot but weak and gradually turning strong and tannic as it stands. Leave the lid off the pot to signal that you want a refill. Green tea is a refreshing alternative.

Soft drinks including international brands are available everywhere.

Beer goes well with most Chinese food. The best-known brand comes from a brewery started a century ago in the German concession of Tsingtao (now Qingdao), but each province makes its own. Big cities have western-style pubs with draught beers.

Imported wines are expensive, but drinkable reds and whites are now being made in China with French or Australian technical assistance. Read labels carefully; the word "wine" can also mean various fermented, fortified or distilled concoctions made from sundry cereals or fruits. At banquets you may be served *maotai*, a colourless spirit made from sorghum. It's supposed to be knocked back in one gulp to the toast of *ganbei* ("empty glass").

113

The Hard Facts

Airports

Most of China's biggest cities, including those on the usual tourist routes, have spacious, modern airports, with signs and announcements in English as well as Mandarin. Major airlines operate flights to Beijing from all over the world. Shanghai, Dalian, Guangzhou and other cities are also served by international flights. Beijing's International Airport (code BJS or PEK) is 26 km (16 miles) northeast of the city centre. Airport buses run to several main hotels; the journey takes about 50 minutes. If your hotel is not served, go to the nearest stop and take a taxi. Taxis are readily available at the airport—use approved cabs from the official line and ensure that their meters are turned on.

Air China is China's major international airline. The biggest domestic carriers are China Southern and China Eastern; they also operate some international routes.

Shanghai's new international airport at Pudong is linked to the city by the world's first maglev (magnetic levitation) frictionless railway.

The departure tax (or Airport Construction Fee), more for international than for domestic flights, is included in the price of your plane ticket. Children up to the age of 12 are exempt).

Hong Kong's Chep Lap Kok airport (code HKG) is a 20-minute ride by express train from Kowloon, longer from Hong Kong Island or by airport bus.

Baggage

On most flights, the allowance for check-in baggage is 20 kg (44 lb). One small carry-on bag is permitted.

Climate

China spreads across a similar range of latitudes to the US, so the climate varies just as much. The north resembles its neighbour Siberia, while the far south is hot and humid for much of the year. The northeast has hot, dry summers, pleasant autumns and bitterly cold, mainly dry winters. Spring is mild but can be rainy.

The central coast has occasional rain at any time of year, hot and humid summers and cool winters. The south has substantial rainfall, long sub-tropical summers and mild winters. April-May and September-October are the best times to visit most parts of China.

Average daily temperatures (°C)			
	Jan	Apr	Jul	Oct
Beijing	−5	13	26	12
Xi'an	−1	14	27	14
Guangzhou	13	22	28	24

Clothing

Take a raincoat or at least an umbrella. In winter (spring too, in the north), you'll need a warm, weatherproof jacket with a hood (or a hat) and gloves. Strong, comfortable shoes are essential for seeing the sights, where a lot of walking is involved. In summer, take light, washable cottons with a light jacket or sweater in case air-conditioning is too fierce.

Except for business, most Chinese people dress quite informally.

Communications

In the big cities, the telephone system is modern and works well. To make an international call to China, dial the international access code followed by 86 and then the area code (without the initial 0) and number.

To make an international call from China, dial 00 and then the country code (1 for US and Canada, 44 for UK, etc), area code and number.

There are plenty of coin- and card-operated phones; different types of cards are sold and are not interchangeable. Check rates before calling; there may be a minimum charge. Local calls are usually free, although hotels may make a charge.

Mobile phones are in widespread use but the system is not compatible with those in some other countries; check with your service provider to see if roaming is available.

It generally costs much more to use the phone in your hotel room, unless you have a calling card issued by international telephone companies. Fax messages can be sent and received through many hotels. Internet access and e-mail service is available at major business-oriented hotels.

Postal services are reliable, although quite slow, especially from remote locations. Airmail reaches most European and North American destinations in 5 to 10 days. Stamps are usually available at hotels as well as post offices.

Driving

Visitors are permitted to drive in China but they must have a local licence, which is not practical for short trips. Cars can be rented only at certain international airports and in major cities, and in any case, a car with a driver costs much the same and avoids problems of navigation, parking and dealing with traffic laws. In principle traffic keeps to the right in China, but the behaviour of other drivers and cyclists can be unpredictable, to say the least. Lights are treated as optional; use of the horn is universal but ineffective. Cities are experiencing ever-worsening rush-hour jams.

Embassies and Consulates

British embassy:
  11 Guanghua Lu,
  Jianguomenwai,
  Beijing 100600;
  tel. (010) 5192 4000
Consulates in Shanghai, Guangzhou and Chongqing.
www.britishembassy.org.cn

US embassy:
  3 Xiushuibei Jie,
  Chaoyang District
  Beijing 100600;
  tel. (010) 6532 3831
Consulates in Chengdu, Guangzhou, Hong Kong, Shanghai and Shenyang.
www.usembassy-china.org.cn

Emergencies

Police   tel. 110
Fire Service tel. 119
Ambulance   tel. 120
In case of serious difficulties, contact your embassy or consulate. They can help with lost passports, but not with lost money or tickets.

Essentials

Sun screen cream (with a high protection factor), sun hat, dark glasses, film and any medicines you may need—the same brands may not be available. Insect repellent is essential in summer. Take lip salve and moisturizer; the air in north China can be very dry, especially in winter.

Etiquette

It's usual to shake hands when meeting people and again when taking leave of them. Punctuality is expected. Feelings are generally kept under control: respect this by showing politeness and patience yourself.

In Chinese names, the surname/family name comes first, so Mr Wu Tingze is addressed as Mr Wu. Women keep their own surnames when they marry. (Some people, such as tour guides, adopt a western-style first name to make it easier for visitors.)

Chinese people may approach you asking if they may practise their English (and most have no ulterior motive). Some are very good linguists and you can have an interesting conversation; others just know a few words.

Formalities

For China (but not Hong Kong), visas are required by all travellers except from certain eastern European and C.I.S. (former Soviet Union) countries. Passports must be valid for at least 6 months. Tour groups may be issued with group visas, in which case they must pass through immigration and emigration controls together.

Local currency may be imported or exported up to the amount of 6,000 yuan in cash. There is no limit on foreign currency, but amounts exceeding 5,000 US$ must be declared on arrival.

You may take the following into China duty-free: 400 cigarettes; 2 bottles (75 cl) of alcoholic drinks; a reasonable quantity of perfume for personal use.

Health and Medical Matters

In summer, use a sunscreen with a high protection factor (at least 15) and make sure that children do the same.

Pharmacies sell a wide variety of medications, but some will be under unfamiliar names, so take an adequate supply with you of any that you need. Intestinal problems (e.g. traveller's diarrhoea) are less likely if you stick to the cooked dishes that are typical of Chinese cuisine and avoid unpeeled fruit, but carry a proprietary medicine with you just in case. Air pollution in cities may affect asthma sufferers. Tap water is not safe to drink unless it has been boiled or treated.

No vaccinations are currently required, but tetanus and typhoid shots are recommended, plus hepatitis and rabies if you are going to leave normal tourist routes to travel in rural and remote areas. There is a risk of malaria in low-lying parts of the southern provinces.

It is advisable to take out comprehensive travel insurance, including coverage of medical expenses. If you need medical attention in China, hotels or CITS/CTS offices can call a doctor or arrange for you to go to a hospital. There is a charge for treatment and for medications. Keep receipts for any payments you have to make, in order to claim refunds.

Language

Mandarin Chinese is the official language, but many regional dialects are spoken, such as Cantonese and Fujianese, so different that they really qualify as separate languages. Then there are the tongues spoken by the various minority peoples: Miao, Yao and Uighur for example.

You will find that Mandarin words written in pinyin are fairly easy to pronounce, but take care with the following consonants:

c is pronounced as **ts** in bi**ts**
g is always hard as in **go**
h is a throaty **ch** as in lo**ch**
j and *zh* are pronounced like the **j** in **j**am
q and *ch* as **ch** in **ch**ill
x and *sh* as **sh** in **sh**all
z as ds in la**ds**

During your visit you will soon become familiar with the following words:

dadao	boulevard
dajie	street
dian	hall
dong	cave
he	river
hu	lake
jiang	river
ling	tomb
lu	road
men	gate
shan	mountain
si	temple
ta	pagoda
tai	terrace
xia	gorge
yuan	garden

These syllables are linked together with the proper noun, so the Li River is written *Lijiang*.

On city maps you will see the words

north	*bei*
south	*nan*
east	*dong*
west	*xi*

combined with *lu* (road) or *jie* (street), to indicate the geographical sector, i.e. Nanjing Donglu and Nanjing Xilu designate the east and west sections of the same thoroughfare.

One particularity of Mandarin is that there are no words equivalent to "yes" and "no". When someone asks a question, the verb is repeated as the answer, together with the word *bu* before the verb if the answer is negative. For instance, the answer to "Do you want a dessert?" would be "Want" *(yao)* instead of "Yes", and "Not want" *(bu yao)* instead of "No".

Sounds complicated? You can always try "OK", universally understood. If you want to break the ice, you could always try: *Ni hui jiang yingyu ma?* (Can you speak English?)—and hope that the reply will be *hui* (Can).

Here are a few more words that may be useful:

I'm…	*wo…*
hungry	*e*
thirsty	*kouke*
tired	*lei*
cold	*juede leng*
hot	*juede re*
right	*youbianr*
left	*zuobianr*
straight on	*yizhi*
opposite	*duimianr*
near	*jin*
far	*yuan*

Media

State-run TV channels are augmented in many hotels by satellite and cable channels, including BBC World, CNN, TV5 and other European channels.

Reception of BBC World Service, Voice of America and other English-language radio stations is generally good on short wave, especially in the evening and early morning.

The official *China Daily* newspaper is available in the cities, at hotels and news-stands. The much livelier Hong Kong newspapers can be found in some major hotels.

Money

The Chinese currency (*renminbi* or "people's money") is the *yuan* (CNY or Y), divided into 10 *jiao* or 100 *fen*, with banknotes from 1 jiao to 100 yuan and coins from 1 fen to 1 yuan.

Hong Kong and Macau have their own currencies. The Hong Kong dollar (HK$) is divided into 100 cents, and the Macau *pataca* (P), divided into 100 *avos*.

Foreign currency and travellers cheques may be changed at banks, exchange offices and the bigger hotels (at much the same rate everywhere). Keep receipts in case you need to change some back (it is not permitted to return more than 50% of the amount exchanged). Yuan are not exchangeable outside China. Even in Hong Kong, only the Bank of China will exchange them, after making a large deduction.

Major credit cards are accepted in the better hotels and in some restaurants and stores used to dealing with foreign customers. ATMs outside big city banks will deliver cash if you have the right card and PIN; check with your bank before leaving home.

Opening Hours

Museums and other attractions generally open from 9 a.m. to about 5 p.m. Some close on Monday. It is worth checking in advance to save a wasted journey.

Shops open daily from 9 a.m. to around 7 p.m. Some local stores open for longer hours.

Offices open Monday to Friday from 8 or 8.30 a.m. to 5 p.m.

Banks open Monday to Friday from 9 a.m. to 4.30 or 5 p.m. Some may close from noon to 1 p.m. Big city main offices may have at least one counter open on Saturdays and Sundays.

Photography and Video

Do not photograph anything that could be construed as a military objective. Photography is also forbidden in many museums and parts of some religious buildings. Ask permission before taking someone's photograph.

Videotape is available. Pre-recorded tapes and DVDs may not be compatible with the system in your home country.

Public Holidays

1 January	New Year's Day
8 March	Women's Day
1 May	Labour Day
4 May	Youth Day (combined with Labour Day as a week's holiday)
1 June	Children's Day

119

1 July	Foundation Day (of Communist Party)
1 August	Army Day
1 October	National Day (extended to a week's holiday)

Moveable:
Chinese New Year (usually late January or February)—a week's holiday.

Public Transport

Taxis are inexpensive and readily available (they can be hailed in the street), but make sure the driver turns on the meter. The charge per kilometre is shown on a sticker in the window; bigger cars charge more. If you take a pedicab (bicycle rickshaw), agree the price in advance. Have your destination written in Chinese before setting out, and the address of the place where you are staying.

Apart from tour buses, buses are cheap but uncomfortable and usually packed, with standing room only.

Beijing, Shanghai and Guangzhou have subway (metro) systems, and other cities are building them. They are easy to use, with colour coding and clear signs in Pinyin as well as Chinese.

Trains are the backbone of the transport system, serving all big cities and towns. In major centres, there are signs and announcements in English. Tickets may be bought at stations or CITS and other travel agents. Express trains cost more than the regular service, and sleeping berths are extra. Foreigners are charged more than local people. Seating is either "soft" (quite comfortable) or "hard" (with little or no padding, and usually very crowded). It is usually necessary to book well in advance to obtain the seats and times you want.

Domestic flights are operated by many different regional carriers, using modern aircraft. Flights are non-smoking; soft drinks, tea and snacks are served. There is rarely an empty seat, so you should make reservations well in advance. Airport announcements are made in English as well as Chinese.

Safety

Crime against foreigners is still rare, although the incidence is increasing. As in every other country, beware of pickpockets in crowded places and take normal precautions: avoid dark or lonely places at night, and don't leave valuable items lying around. Use hotel safes.

Time

All of China is on GMT + 8 (UTC + 8), despite its enormous size. The far west compensates by adjusting working hours to correspond with daylight.

Tipping

Until recent years tipping was officially banned, but the practice has been growing, especially in the expanding private sector.

A service charge is usually included in restaurant bills; no tip is expected. Porters are tipped up to 5 yuan per bag, depending on the standard of hotel. Taxi fares may be rounded up by a small amount.

Toilets

Public lavatories are of the hole-in-the-ground variety, and generally in a filthy state. Restaurants have much better facilities, as do some tourist attractions. A small charge is sometimes levied, which may mean slightly higher standards. Toilet paper is rarely provided.

Tourist Information

All major cities have a China International Travel Service (CITS) office, generally open Monday to Friday 9 a.m.–5 p.m. Some of them have information leaflets and maps of the local area. The better hotels may also have local tourist information.

The China National Tourist Office (CNTO) has two offices in the US, and can provide brochures before you leave home:

350 Fifth Avenue, Suite 6413
New York, NY 10118
tel. 1 212-760 9700
fax 1 212-760 8809

600 West Broadway. Suite 320
Glendale, Los Angeles
CA 91204
tel. (818) 545 7507
fax (818) 545 7506

Voltage

The electrical supply is 220V, 50 Hz, AC. Plugs are of various types: European (two round pins); British (three square pins); US (two flat); or Australasian (angled flat pins). Carry a universal adaptor if you want to be sure you can plug in your appliances. Apart from shavers for which a marked outlet is provided, any 110V equipment needs a transformer as well as an adaptor.

Water

The tap water is *not* safe to drink (except in some of the top class hotels). Stick to bottled water, spring, filtered or distilled, which is widely available, at an astonishing range of prices (from roughly 1 yuan/litre to—well, the sky's the limit, depending on what the vendor thinks the market will stand). Check that the seal is unbroken.

Many hotels provide flasks of boiled water, and also electric kettles.

121

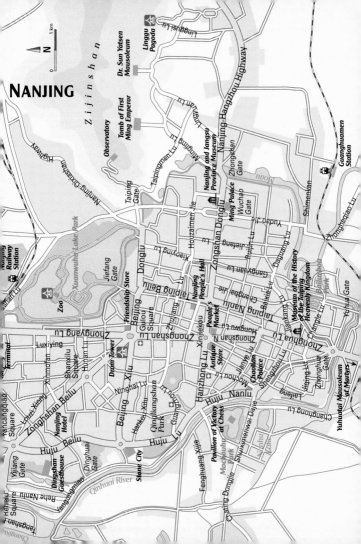

NANJING

Zijinshan

Linggu Pagoda

Dr. Sun Yatsen Mausoleum

Tomb of First Ming Emperor

Observatory

Linggu Lu

Nanjing-Hangzhou Highway

Nanjing and Jangsu Province Museum

Zhongshan Gate

Guanghuamen Station

Ming Palace

Wuchap Gate

Shimenkan

Nanjing-Dashanan Highway

Taiping Gate

Taiping Lu

Zhongshan Donglu

Jiefang Gate

Xuanwuhai Lake Park

Friendship Store

Zoo

Dongilu

Beilu

Zhongshan

Xiaoying Lu

Houzaimen Jie

Nanjing People's Hall

People's Market

Zhongshan Beilu

Gulou Square

Hunan Lu

Museum of the History of the Taiping Heavenly Kingdom

Taiping Nanlu

Ruijinlu

Yuhua Gate

Zhongyang Lu

Drum Tower

Luxiying

Shankilu Square

Xinmofan

Shanxi-Xiang

Zhongshan Beilu

Ninghai Lu

Zhongshan Lu

Xinjiekou

Antique Store

Hanzhong Lu

Chaotian Palace

Nanlu

Zhonghua Gate

Yuhuatai Mausoleum of Martyrs

Nanjing Hotel

Beijing

Hankou Xilu

Qinjiangshan Park

Huju Lu

Huju Lu

Pavilion of Victory at Chess

Stone City

Mochouhu Park

Qinhuai River

Dingshan Guesthouse

Dinghuai Gate

Yangzhongmiao

Yijiang Gate

Changjiang

Tsanglagiao

Yancang Square

Huju Beilu

Rehe Nanlu

Yangzi

Tianren Square

Changjiang

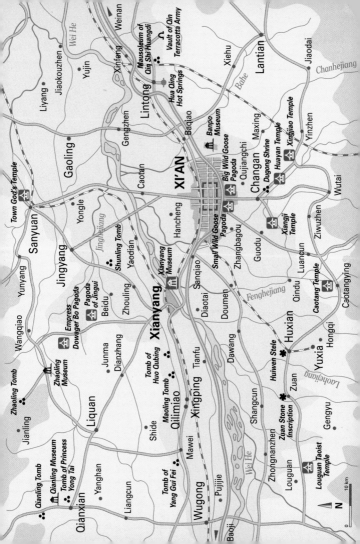

INDEX

Airports 114
Badaling Pass 26
Baidicheng 58
Banpo Stone Age
Village 39
Bargaining 107
Beidaihe 30–31
Beijing 17–24
  Beihai Park 22
  Bell Towers 21–22
  Chairman Mao
  Memorial Hall 19
  Drum Towers
  21–22
  Forbidden City
  19–22
  Hall of Prayer for a
  Good Harvest 23
  Halls of Harmony
  20–21
  Heroes' Memorial
  19
  Hutong district 22
  Imperial
  Collections 21
  Imperial Garden 21
  Imperial Vault of
  Heaven 23
  Jingshan Park 21
  Old Summer
  Palace 23–24
  Summer Palace
  23
  Temple of Heaven
  22–23
  Tiananmen
  Square 18–19
  Zoo 24

Chengde 27–30
Chengdu 60
Cheung Chau 96
Chongqing 59
Climate 114–115
Clothing 115
Coloane 101
Communications 115
Consulates 116
Cuiheng 80
Dali 64
Dalian 31–33
Daning River 55–57
Dian Lake 63
Driving 115–116
Dujiangyan 61
Dunhuang 44
Embassies 116
Emeishan 61
Etiquette 111, 116
Famen Temple 43
Fengdu 59
Fengjie 58–59
Formalities 116
Foshan 80
Gezhou Dam 52–53
Grand Canal 73
Great Wall 26–27
Guangzhou 77–79
  Chen Family
  Temple 79
  Flower Pagoda 78
  Huaisheng
  Mosque 78
  Qingping Market 79
  Revolutionary
  Memorials 79
  Yuexiu Park 78

Guilin 83–84
Gulangyu 87
Haikou 82
Hainan Island 81–83
Hangzhou 74–75
Health 117
Hong Kong 89–96
Hong Kong Island
  91–94
Huangshan 49
Huaqing Hot
  Springs 42
Jade 102
Jingzhou 51–52
Jinshanling Pass 27
Kashgar 45
Kat Hing Wai 96
Kowloon 94–95
Kuimen 57–58
Kunming 62–63
Lake Tai 74
Lamma 96
Language 102–103,
  117–118
Lantau 96
Laoshan 35
Leshan 61
Li River 84–85
Lijiang 63–64
Macau 99–101
Mai Po Marshes
  96
Media 118–119
Ming Tombs 24–26
Money 119
Mount Putuo 75
Mutianyu 27
Nanjing 47–48

New Territories 95–96
Ningbo 75
Opening Hours 119
Opera 103–104
Panda Research Centre 60
Photography 119
Public holidays 119–120
Public transport 120
Qingdao 33–35
Radiant Crag Lake 81
Religion 104–105
Safety 120
Shamian Island 79–80
Shanghai 65–70
  Bund 65–66
  Grand Theatre 68
  Historical Villas 69
  Huangpu Park 66
  Jade Buddha Temple 68–70
  Nanjing Road 68
  Shanghai Museum 68
  Old City 68
  Old Market 68
  Pudong 66
  Peace Hotel 66
  Yuyuan Garden 68
Shatin 95–96
Shilin Stone Forest 63
Silk 105

Silk Road 43–45
Suzhou 70–71
Taipa 101
Tang Tombs 42–43
Terracotta Warriors 40–42
Three Gorges Dam 52, 53
Tianjin 30
Time 120–121
Tipping 121
Toilets 121
Tourist information 121
Turpan 44–45
Urumqi 44
Voltage 121
Wanxian 59
Water 121
Wenchang 82
Western Hills 63
Wu Gorge 54–55
Wuhan 50
Wushan 55
Wuxi 71–74
Xi'an 36–42
Xiamen 85–87
Xianyang 42–43
Xiling Gorge 53–54
Xishuangbanna 64
Yangtze Bridge 47
Yangtze river cruises 50–59
Yantai 33
Yichang 52
Yueyang 51
Zhanjiang 80–81
Zijinshan 48–49

GENERAL EDITOR
Barbara Ender-Jones
YANGTZE SECTION
Damian Harper
LAYOUT
Luc Malherbe
PHOTO CREDITS
Hémisphères/Gardel, pp. 1, 5, 6, 15, 16, 20, 25, 28, 34, 40, 72, 104, 108, 113; /Gotin, p. 2; /Rabouan, pp. 60–61; /Cintract pp. 64, 98; /Nicolas, p. 92; /Barbier, p 103;
B. Joliat, pp. 11, 82, 85, 97;
L. Minder, pp. 31, 36–37;
Christine Osborne Pictures, pp. 45, 100, 110;
C. Vaschetto, pp. 46, 56;
R.J.Stevens, p. 67;
N. Setchfield, p. 68;
Bildagentur Baumann/Kanus, p. 76; /Hiroshi Higuchi, p. 95;
F. Fontaine, p. 88
MAPS
Elsner & Schichor;
JPM Publications

Copyright © 2006, 2002 by JPM Publications S.A. 12, avenue William-Fraisse, 1006 Lausanne, Switzerland
information@jpmguides.com
http://www.jpmguides.com/

Printed in Switzerland – 05/10/02
Weber/Bienne
Edition 2006